B'ajlom ii Nkotz'i'j .

Yucatec Maya
Phrasebook

Ideal for Traveling in La Península de Yucatán,
México

Convenient Travel Size

Mateo G. Russo and Sandra Chigüela

(2018)

Dedicated to my beautiful wife Sandra and our four beautiful children Cristel, Emilio Carlos, Alejandra and Camila.

MGR

Brief History of the Author

Mateo Russo and his wife Sandra founded 'Bajlom ii Nkotz'i'j Publications' in 2018. The organization was named using two words of Mayan origin from the Tz'utujiil Language of Guatemala. The two words tell the love story of Mateo and Sandra. 'B'ajlom' means 'Jaguar' and the word 'Nkotz'i'j' means 'My flower' which is the loving name that Mateo gave to his wife. This love story of the Jaguar and his beloved flower gave birth to the mission of Mateo to preserve indigenous languages of Guatemala and southern Mexico and to create linguistic texts that can provide a written record of specific dialects and the stories of people who are collaborators with this project. The goal is to preserve all of the indigenous languages of Guatemala and others from southern Mexico; not only through a text book or grammar book, but through poetry, songs, and many other forms of literary art and artistic expression. The goal is to give a voice to the highly marginalized indigenous people who have been highly discriminated against in all societies of Latin America. Mateo has hopes in expanding this project through time, one language at a time. Mateo's philosophy is founded in the philosophy of EZLN (The Zapatista Army of National Liberation) and through the teachings of Subcomandante Marcos the original spokesperson for EZLN. The fight of EZLN has inspired Mateo to create another front in the fight that continues: The battle to preserve and protect the remnants of our past and our perception of the world around us, our own words and those words being of our ancestors. Our indigenous linguistic history is very beautiful and it needs to be preserved, because it is our linguistic inheritance. Despite that many indigenous languages are moribund... Mateo and his wife have joined together with the fight to preserve the most important facet of the cultures of the indigenous people: Our linguistic inheritance (our mother tongues). Mateo passionately supports Indigenous Human Rights and the preservation and protection of every indigenous language of Guatemala and southern Mexico. Mateo will not rest until every indigenous language has a written literary archive and until the voice of the indigenous people is not forgotten but is permanently marked in human history.

Contact Information:

'B'ajlom ii Nkotz'i'j Publications'

biinpublications@gmail.com

biinpublications@facebook.com

If you would like to donate to our cause and give your support or if you would like to donate your time or be a literary collaborator with us, please, contact us by e-mail.

Section Guide for Phrasebook

A) Basic Yucatec Maya Grammar:

I)   Yucatec Maya Alphabet and Pronunciation

        a. Vowels

II)   Personal Pronouns

III)   Prepositions with Pronouns: Yetel (With) and Ti' (To; At; On; In)

IV)   The Noun

V)   The Adjective

VI)   Definitive and indefinitive articles

VII)   This and That

VIII)   Interrogatives

IX)   Sentence Structure

X)   Verbs (Present, Past and Future)

XI)   I to you and You to me

XII)   Verbal Adjectives and Passive Voice

XIII)   Negation: Ma'...-i

XIV)   Commands [imperatives]

XV)   Commands with negation

XVI)   Subjunctive

XVII)   Oneself = (#) + BA

XVIII) Adverbs, Conjunctions and
Prepositions

B) Phrasebook:

I)   Hello's and Goodbye's

II)   Basic phrases of Conversation

III)   Common Commands [Imperatives]

IV)   Emergency Phrases

V)   Numbers

C)   Useful Yucatec Maya Vocabulary

Food

Animals

People

Places

Nature

Other Important Words

Common Adjectives

The Body

Clothing

Colors

Common Verbs

Brief Grammar Guide to the Yucatec Maya Language:

The Yucatec Maya Language called 'Maayat'aan' by its native speakers, is the most widely spoken Mayan Language of the Mayan Language Linguistic Family. The largest populations of Yucatec Maya native speakers are amassed in La Península de Yucatán, México and, as well, in Campeche, Quintana Roo and in isolated areas of Belize. There are also substantial communities of Yucatec Maya native speakers in Péten, Guatemala. Maayat'aan literally means "Speech of the Maya," as the people who speak the language refer to themselves as "the Maya." Of course, this term is used loosely by all anthropologists and linguists for all Mayan Languages within the Mayan Language Linguistic

Family; for example – Tz' utujiil Maya, Kaqchikel Maya, Mam Maya, K'iche' Maya, etc. Each individual cultural group has its own name and cultural heritage without the agroupation of their individual cultures under one Mayan Culture. When 'Maya' is used by Anthropologists or Linguists it usually refers to the Linguistic Family as a whole and does not refer to one specific group. In general, 'Maya' refers to the Yucatec people and their culture.

This publication will give the reader a base with the Yucatec Language on which to expound; whether during self-study or with the use of this publication as a tool in the field. The dialect used within this publication is primarily the dialect of La Península de Yucatán, México; including variances from other regions.

I)   Basic Yucatec Maya (Maayat'aan) Grammar

The Yucatec Maya Alphabet and Pronunciation

Yucatec Maya letters are pronounced in the same manner as they are in Spanish. Therefore, Spanish speakers already have an advantage, but only with few exceptions which are discussed in the notes after the first displayed alphabet:

A a

B b

Ch ch

Ch' ch'[1]

E e

I i

J j[3]

K k

K' k'[1]

L l

M m

N n

O o

P p

R r

S s

T t

Ts ts⁴

Tz' tz'¹&⁴

U u

W w

X x²

Y y

' ¹

1) These letters have a brief glottal stop after the initial consonant; with all simplicity it is a brief pause, as well, this brief glottal stop can be located in various parts of Yucatec words.
2) X x is pronounced like (sh) as in 'shopping'
3) J j is pronounced the same as in Spanish; like a rough (h).
4) Tz tz, Tz' tz' are pronounced like (Dz).

The following is a step-by-step pronunciation guide of the Yucatec alphabet for native speakers of English:

A a – has the sound value of the 'a' in 'awe' or the 'o' in 'pot'; at times depending where it is in a word it can have the sound value of 'u' in 'mud'

B b – has the sound value of 'b' in 'bat'.

Ch ch – has the sound value of 'ch' in 'church'.

Ch' ch' – has the sound value of 'ch' in 'church'; but with a brief glottal stop after the letter.

E e – has the sound value of 'e' in 'bet'; is represented in this book with 'eh'

I i – has the sound value of 'ee' in 'beet'. Same as Spanish pronounciation.

J j – has the same sound value of the 'j' in Spanish. Sounds like a rough 'h'. In this book this sound is expressed with 'H'.

K k – has the sound value of 'c' in 'cot' or 'conch'.

K' k' – has the same sound value as 'k', but followed by a brief glottal stop.

L l – has the sound value of 'l' in 'lamb'.

M m – has the same sound value of 'm' in 'man'.

N n – has the same sound value of 'n' in 'not'.

O o – has the sound value of 'oa' in 'boat'.

P p – has the sound value of 'p' in 'potato'

R r – has the same sound value as 'r' in 'run'.

S s – has the same sound value as 's' in 'song'.

T t – has the same sound value as 't' in 'top'

Tz tz – has the sound value of 'DZ'.

Tz' tz' - has the sound value of 'DZ' followed by a brief glottal stop.

U u – has the sound value of 'oo' in 'boot'.

W w – has the sound value of 'w' in 'water'.

X x – has the sound value of 'sh' or 'ʃ' in 'shrimp' or 'shore'.

Y y – has the sound value of 'y' in 'yak'.

' - brief glottal stop...can be in various placements in a noun or verb. The best way to explain the sound value is the space between: 'uh-oh'. It is like taking a quick breath between letters.

I (a) Vowels

A, E, I, O, U

- Vowels without stress [aw, ay, ee, oh, oo]

There are instances in the Yucatec Language that vowels may be paired with 'J,' thus, giving them a rough 'h' sound similar to that of Spanish, following the initial vowel. Sometimes, the vowel used may be doubled based on the length of the vowel and, as well, may have the rough 'h' sound along with the doubled vowel.

- AA, EE, II, OO, UU
- AJ, EJ, IJ, OJ, UJ
- AAJ, EEJ, IIJ, OOJ, UUJ

In other rare occurences there may be a diphthong such as:

- UW
- EW

This although rare will have the sound value of 'oof / oov' and 'ef / ev,' where the 'w' will sound very much like a 'f' or 'v.'

II)   Personal Pronouns

In this part there are two tables; Set A is used with nouns and verbs and consists of a prefix and with plural forms there is a suffix, as well. Set B always is used as a suffix and can be used to make a noun or adjective into a verbal construction, it can be used as a direct object at the end of a verbal construction which would include Set A prefixes and, as well, is used with prepositions; especially 'yetel (with)' and 'ti (to; at; on; in).'

SET A AFFIXES

First person singular and plural	IN *(W-) = I	K- IN *(W-)...O'ON K-...-E'EX = WE
Second person singular and plural	A *(W-) = YOU	A *(W-)...-E'EX = YOU ALL
Third person singular and plural	U *(Y-) = HE, SHE, IT	U *(Y-)...O'OB = THEY

*IF A VERBAL ROOT BEGINS WITH A VOWEL THERE ARE PREFIXES ADDED TO THE STEM THAT COINCIDE WITH THE APPROPRIATE PRONOUN.

EXAMPLE:

-AANTIK = TO HELP

+

IN W-

=

M'IN K'AAT IN WAANTIKEECH –

I DON'T WANT TO HELP YOU

SET B AFFIXES

1st pers. sing. and plural	-EEN = I / ME	-O'ON = WE / US
2nd pers. sing. and plural	-EECH = YOU / YOU	-E'EX = YOU ALL / YOU ALL
3rd pers. sing. and plural	-I / -E = (HE, SHE / HIM, HER)	-O'OB = THEY / THEM

SET B CAN BE USED TO CONVERT NOUNS AND ADJECTIVES INTO STATEMENTS ABOUT THE SUBJECT; ABOUT EITHER ONESELF OR SOMEONE ELSE (SEE NOUNS AND ADJECTIVES).

SET B IS ALSO USED TO EXPRESS DIRECT OBJECTS AND ARE PLACED AT THE END OF THE VERBAL STRUCTURE.

Examples:

IN WATAN = My Wife

A WAAMIIGO = Your companion

YOTOCH = His / Her house

IN WOTOCH = My house

A MIIS = Your cat

U K'ABA' = His name

YETELO'ON = With us

KIN YAKUNTIKEECH = I love you

¿KU PAATAL A WAANTIKEEN? =
Can you help me?

WINIKEEN = I am a man

U WAAJO'OB = Their tortillas

JATZ'UTZEECH = You are beautiful

III) Prepositions: Yetel (With) and Ti' (To; At; On; In)

Here are examples of the prefixes and the infixes used with prepositions:

YETEL = WITH

1	YETELEEN (With me)	YETELO'ON (With us)	
2	YETELEECH (With you)	YETELE'EX (With you all)	
3	YETELE (With him, her)	YETELO'OB (With them)	

TI' = TO; AT; ON; IN

1	TEEN (To me)	TO'ON (To us)
2	TEECH (To you)	TE'EX (To you all)
3	TI'E / LEETI' (To him, her, it)	TI'O'OB / LETI'O'OB (To them)

Examples:

¿A k'aat binel yeteleen? (Do you want to go with me?)

¿Ba'ax tz'a wa'alik *leeti'? (What did you say to him?)

*Ti' (to...) [Teen, Teech, Ti'e / Leeti', To'on, Te'ex, Ti'o'ob / Leeti'o'ob]

OTHER COMMON PREPOSITIONS:

-UTI'A'AL = FOR

-YOK'OL = OVER; ABOVE

-YAANAL = UNDER

-TU = BESIDE; AT THE SIDE OF

-CHUUMUK = IN THE MIDDLE OF; AMONG

IV) The Noun

Basic nouns:

Ba'alche' (Wild Animal)

Aalak' (Domestic Animal)

Beel (Road, Path)

Waaj (tortilla)

Xch'uup (Woman)

Maak/ Wiinik / Xiib (Man)

K'iin (Day / Sun)

Otoch (Home / House)

Atan (Wife)

Peek' (Dog)

Janal (Food)

O'och (Food / Tortilla)

Miis (Cat)

Kaan (Snake)

Xch'uupaal (Young Girl)

Cheba (Beer)

Jatz'utziil (Beauty)

Bu'ul (Bean / Beans)

Boxja' (Coffee)

Xi'im (Corn)

Witz (Mountains)

All nouns in their plural form take the ending:

-OB (PLURAL SUFFIX / -O'OB (PLURAL SUFFIX

*WITHIN THIS PUBLICATION I TEND TO USE -OB WITH NOUNS AND -O'OB WITH VERBAL CONSTRUCTIONS OR PRONOUNS THAT INDICATE THE 3RD PERSON PLURAL. HOWEVER, THE EMPHASIZED SOUND VALUE OF -O'OB IS FAR MORE ACCURATE THAN -OB. THE IMPLEMENTATION OF -OB IS SIMPLY USED TO HELP THE READER DISTINGUISH THE USE OF THIS PLURAL SUFFIX AMOUNG NOUNS AND WITHIN VERBAL CONSTRUCTIONS.

WAAJOB – TORTILLAS

WIINIKOB – MEN

XCH'UUPOB – WOMEN

XCH'UUPAALOB – GIRLS

PEEK'OB – DOGS

WITZOB – MOUNTAINS

XIIBOB – MEN

MAAKOB – MEN

OTOCHOB – HOUSES

CHE'OB – TREES

MIISOB – CATS

KAANOB – SNAKES

K'IINOB – DAYS

All nouns receive Set A affixes to indicate possession of the noun:

IN K'ABA' – MY NAME

A K'ABA' – YOUR NAME

U K'ABA' – HIS / HER NAME

IN WAAJ – MY TORTILLA

A WAAJ – YOUR TORTILLA

K WAAJ – OUR TORTILLA

U WAAJO'OB – THEIR TORTILLA

A WAAJE'EX – YOUR TORTILLA [TWO OR MORE PEOPLE]

IN PEEK' – MY DOG

U PEEK' – HIS / HER DOG

When the noun begins with a vowel, additions are added along with the original affix:

IN WATAN – MY WIFE

A WATAN – YOUR WIFE

U YATAN – HIS WIFE

IN WOTOCH – MY HOUSE

A WOTOCH – YOUR HOUSE

U YOTOCH – HIS / HER HOUSE

KOTOCH – OUR HOUSE

A WOTOCHE'EX – YOUR HOUSE [TWO OR MORE PEOPLE]

U YOTOCHO'OB – THEIR HOUSE

Usually in spoken form, some of these may lose their initial form from Set A:

YATAN – HIS WIFE

YOTOCH – HIS / HER HOUSE

YOTOCHO'OB – THEIR HOUSE

Short stem nouns will take a '-il' ending when they have a possessive pronoun:

NAJ – HOUSE

+ -IL =

POSSESSIVE PRONOUN + NAJIIL

A NAJIIL = YOUR HOUSE

IN NAJIIL = MY HOUSE

U NAJIIL = HIS / HER HOUSE

With Set B suffixes a noun can be made into a verb or to create a statement and, as well, can be used to convert adjectives in a similar fashion (see Adjectives); usually indicating that the speaker is related to or has relation to the word with the affix:

WIINIKEEN = I AM A MAN

WIINIKEECH = YOU ARE A MAN

WIINIKI = HE IS A MAN

WIINIKO'ON = WE ARE MEN

WIINIKE'EX = YOU ALL ARE MEN

WIINIKO'OB = THEY ARE MEN

XCH'UUPEEN = I AM A WOMAN

XCH'UUPEECH = YOU ARE A WOMAN

XCH'UUPI = SHE IS A WOMAN

XCH'UUPO'ON = WE ARE WOMEN

XCH'UUPE'EX = YOU ALL ARE WOMEN

XCH'UUPO'OB = THEY ARE WOMEN

KATUUNEEN = I AM A SOLDIER

KATUUNEECH = YOU ARE A SOLDIER

KATUUNI = HE / SHE IS A SOLDIER

CHAMPALEEN = I AM A CHILD

CHAMPALEECH = YOU ARE A CHILD

CHAMPALI = HE / SHE IS A CHILD

V)   The Adjective

Adjectives are always located before the nouns and not afterwards like in Spanish.

NOJOCH (Big)

NUUKTAK (Big)

CH'UJUK (Sweet)

TUUMBEN (New)

JATZ'UTZ (Beautiful)

UTZ (Good)

K'AAS (Bad, Evil)

CHAN (Small)

CHICHAN (Small)

MEJEN (Small)

CHOKOJ (Hot)

K'IINAAL (Hot)

SIIS (Cold)

POLOK (Fat)

TZ'OYA'AN (Skinny)

PAAP (Spicy)

*KI'IMAK OOL (Happy)

K'A'ANA'AN (Important)

KUXA'AN (Alive)

EEK' (Dirty)

JAANIIL (Clean)

SAAK (Clean)

EE'JOCH'E'EN (Obscure, Dark)

NOOKOY (Cloudy)

AL (Heavy)

YAJ (Difficult)

PIIM (Thick)

Examples:

JATZ'UTZ XCH'UUP = Beautiful Woman

TZ'OYA'AN PAAL = Skinny Boy

PAAP JAANAL = Spicy Food

LE JAANALO' PAAP = The Food is Spicy

LE XCH'UUPO' JATZ'UTZ = The Woman is Beautiful

LE PAALO' TZ'OYA'AN = The Boy is Skinny

*KI'IMAK -OOL = RECEIVES THE SET A
AFFIXES THAT PRECEDE VOWELS 'IN W...'

KI'IMAK IN WOOL = I AM CONTENT / HAPPY

An adjective can be used to describe oneself or another person when a suffix from the Set B is used. Usually this form is used with making a statement.

JATZ'UTZEEN = I am beautiful

JATZ'UTZEECH = You are beautiful

JATZ'UTZI = He / She is beautiful

JATZ'UTZE'EX = You all are beautiful

JATZ'UTZO'OB = They are beautiful

K'OJA'ANEEN = I am sick

K'OJA'ANEECH = You are sick

K'OJA'ANI = He / She is sick

K'OJA'ANO'ON = We are sick

K'OJA'ANE'EX = You all are sick

TZ'OYA'ANEEN = I am skinny

TZ'OYA'ANEECH = You are skinny

TZ'OYA'ANI = He / She is skinny

TZ'OYA'ANE'EX = You all are skinny

TZ'OYA'ANO'OB = They are skinny

KUXA'ANEEN = I am alive

KUXA'ANEECH = You are alive

KUXA'ANI = He / She is alive

KUXA'ANO'ON = We are alive

KUXA'ANE'EX = You all are alive

KUXA'ANO'OB = They are alive

POLOKEEN = I am fat

POLOKEECH = You are fat

POLOKI = He / She is fat

POLOKO'ON = We are fat

POLOKE'EX = You all are fat

POLOKO'OB = They are fat

ADJECTIVES CAN ALSO BE CONVERTED INTO VERBS:

JATZ'UTZ = BEAUTIFUL; PRETTY; CUTE

JATZ'UTZIIL = BEAUTY

-TAL = STATE OF BECOMING OR BEING SOMETHING

IN THE CASE OF ADJECTIVES BEING MADE INTO VERBS, THIS WOULD MEAN A CHANGE FROM ONE STATE TO ANOTHER OR TO BECOME SOMETHING DIFFERENT THAN BEFORE:

JATZ'UTZTAL = TO BECOME BEAUTIFUL

VERBAL CONJUGATION:

PRESENT:

TIN JATZ'UTZTAL = I AM BECOMING BEAUTIFUL

PAST TENSE:

JATZ'UTZCHAJEEN = I BECAME BEAUTIFUL

VI) Definitive Articles and Indefinitive Articles

There are no Definite Articles in the Yucatec Language. Instead it is expressed with "This / That" which form around nouns and, as well, are sentence markers that show the difference between the Subject and the Object of the sentence:

INDEPENDENT FORMS:

LELO' = THAT

LELA' = THIS

DEPENDENT FORMS:

PEEK' = DOG

LE PEEKO' = THAT DOG

LE PEEKA' = THIS DOG

LE ...O' = THAT

LE ...A' = THIS

In the Yucatec Language, the use of Indefinite Articles is implemented as they are in the English Language or the Spanish Language. The use of 'a' or 'an' is common with nouns, but may receive a classifier suffix preceded by a numerical value, which in this case is used to express the Indefinite Article:

JUN (ONE; A, AN)

JUN + P'EL = JUMP'EL (A, AN; ONE OF SOMETHING; GENERAL CLASSIFIER)

Here is a short list of Classifiers that will be used based on whether the noun is something animate or inanimate or something even more specific:

-P'EL = IN GENERAL; CAN BE USED WITH ANYTHING

-P'IIT = A LITTLE OF SOMETHING OR A SMALL QUANTITY OF THE FOLLOWING NOUN

-KUUL = TREE

-TUUL = PERSON OR ANIMAL; ANIMATE

-TZ'IIT = SOMETHING LONG; OR THIN AND LONG

JUMP'EL = ONE THING

JUMP'IIT = A LITTLE BIT OF SOMETHING

JUNKUUL = ONE TREE

JUNTUUL = ONE PERSON OR ONE ANIMAL

JUNTZ'IIT = ONE THING THAT IS LONG AND SLENDER

JUMP'EL CHEBA = ONE BEER; A BEER

JUMP'IIT O'OCH = A LITTLE BIT OF FOOD; SOME FOOD

JUNKUUL CHE' = ONE TREE; A TREE

JUNTUUL XCH'UUP = ONE WOMAN; A WOMAN

JUNTZ'IIT CHE' = ONE STICK (FROM TREE); A STICK (FROM A TREE)

Examples:

Le Wiiniko' tz'u beetik = That man did it

Le Xch'uupo' tz'u tz'iibtik = That woman wrote it

La Paala' mu' k'aat u binel = This boy does not want to go

In k'aat in manik lelo' = I want to buy that

M'in k'aat in manik lela' = I don't want to buy this

Tza' teen jump'el cheba = Give me a beer

Tz'in wilik juntuul xch'uup = I saw a woman

Kulchajeen naatz' junkuul nojoch che' = I sat next to a large tree

In k'aat jump'iit o'och = I want a little bit of food

VII) This and That

'This' and 'That' are expressed as shown in the previous chapter and can be used in place of 'the.' They indicate whether something is near and in reach or at a distance or away from the speaker.

INDEPENDENT FORMS:

LELO' = THAT

LELA' = THIS

DEPENDENT FORMS:

PEEK' = DOG

LE PEEKO' = THAT DOG

LE PEEKA' = THIS DOG

Examples:

Le Wiiniko' tz'u beetik = That man did it

Le Xch'uupo' tz'u tz'iibtik = That woman wrote it

La Paala' mu' k'aat u binel = This boy does not want to go

In k'aat in manik lelo' = I want to buy that

M'in k'aat in manik lela' = I don't want to buy this

VIII) Interrogatives

Interrogatives in the Yucatec language are as follows:

¿Tu'ux? = Where? To / From where?

¿Ba'ax k'iin? = When? What day?

¿Ba'ax oora? = When? What hour?

¿Bajuux? = How much?

¿B'ix? = How?

¿Ba'ax? = What?

¿Ba'axten? = Why?

¿Maakalmaak...? = What kind of (such)...?

¿Maaxi'? = Who?

¿Maaxi' yetel? = With whom?

Examples:

¿Tu'ux yaan a wotoch? = Where is your house?

¿Ba'axten ka p'ektikeen? = Why do you hate me?

¿Maakalmaak meyaj ka beetik? = What do you do for a living?

¿Maaxi' yetel tz'a bin? = With whom did you go?

¿B'ix yaanileech? = How are you?

¿Bajuux u tojol? = How much does it cost?

¿Ba'ax oora tz'a k'uchul? = When (What time) did you arrive?

IX) Sentence Structure

The construction of the Yucatec phrase is very varied and does not have strict rules, but for the sake of not making this section complicated or overwhelming, the following examples will be demonstrated. The order of Subject, Object and the Verb can vary based on the speaker and almost in all cases the "Le...o'/a'" forms are used to indicate who or what is the subject and who or what is the object of the sentence.

S-V-O / S-O-V / V-S-O, etc.

The structure of the phrase has many options:

Le Wiiniko' tz'u tz'u'utzik le Xch'uupa' =

(That / The) Man kissed (This / The) Woman

(S – V – O)

Le Wiiniko' le Xch'uupa' tz'u tz'u'utzik =

[The fact that that man kissed this woman remains the same]

(S – O – V)

Tz'u Tz'u'utzik le Wiiniko' le Xch'uupa' =

[The fact that that man kissed this woman remains the same]

(V – S – O)

All of the phrases have the same meaning:

The (That) man kissed the (This) woman

X)   Verbs (Present, Past and Future)

There are three main tenses in the Yucatec Language: Present, Past and Future. The structure of the verbs is as follow:

TZ'IIB = TO WRITE

T (Present tense non-habitual) + IN (I) + TZ'IIB (verbal root = to write) = TIN TZ'IIB (I write [non-specific])

The Present...T- (prefix that indicates present tense): Verbal root – Binel (to Go) [Irregular Verb]

1	TIN BIN (I GO)	TANK BIN (WE GO) PL
2	TAN BIN (YOU GO)	TAN BINE'EX (YOU ALL GO) PL
3	TUN BIN (HE, SHE, IT GOES)	TUN BINO'OB (THEY GO) PL

Examples:

Tin bin ti' u yotoch in yuum = I am going to my father's house

Tan janaal jach ya'ab waaj = You eat lots of tortillas

The Habitual Present ...K- (prefix that indicates that the action is habitual or this form is used with questions and interrogatives): Verbal root – Binel (to go) [Irregular Verb]

1	KIN BIN	K BIN
	(I GO)	(WE GO) PL
2	KA BIN	KA BINE'EX
	(YOU GO)	(YOU ALL GO) PL
3	KU BIN	KU BINO'OB
	(HE / SHE GOES)	(THEY GO) PL

Examples:

¿Tu'ux ka bin? = Where are you going?

¿Kin bin ti' in wochoch = I am going home

¿Ba'ax ka beetik? = What are you doing?

Kin beetik lela' ka'aj kin meyaj = I do this when I work

The past tense is somewhat complicated and there are four main ways to express the past tense or completive aspect. Two ways to express the completion of an action are through the implementation of Set B affixes as long as the verb is intransitive. While Transitive verb stems that end in '-ik' receive a different conjugation and ending. Another common form of expressing a completed action is through an auxiliary, which will be explained in more detail in a later chapter.

The Past Tense with Set B affixes (suffix is added to an intransitive verbal root to indicate a completed action)

K'UCHUL = ARRIVE (INTRANSITIVE VERB)

K'UCH | UL

K'UCH + SET B AFFIX

K'UCHEEN = I ARRIVED (COMPLETED ACTION)

K'UCHEECH = YOU ARRIVED (COMPLETED ACTION)

JAANAL = EAT (INTRANSITIVE VERB)

JAAN | AL

JAAN + SET B AFFIX

JAANEEN = I ATE (COMPLETED ACTION)

JAANEECH = YOU ATE (COMPLETED ACTION)

BIN / BINEL = TO GO (IRREGULAR VERB)

1	BINEEN (I WENT)	BINO'ON (WE WENT) PL
2	BINEECH (YOU WENT)	BINE'EX (YOU ALL WENT) PL
3	BINI / BINE (HE, SHE, IT WENT)	BINO'OB (THEY WENT) PL

COMPLETIVE ASPECT WITH TRANSITIVE VERBS:

VERBS THAT END IN '-IK' ARE TRANSITIVE VERBS

-IK IS REMOVED FROM THE VERBAL STEM AND REPLACED WITH -AJ

BEETIK = TO DO SOMETHING

BEET | IK

BEET + AJ

TIN BEETAJ = I DID IT

1	TIN BEETAJ (I DID IT)	*T BEETAJ (WE DID IT) PL
2	TA BEETAJ (YOU DID IT)	TA BEETAJE'EX (YOU ALL DID IT) PL
3	TU BEETAJ (HE /SHE DID IT)	TU BEETAJO'OB (THEY DID IT) PL

*FIRST PERSON PLURAL HAS TWO FORMS IN THIS CASE:

T BEETAJ = WE DID IT

TIN BEETAJO'ON = WE DID IT

WITH AUXILIARY: TZ'OK (ALREADY
ACCOMPLISHED; COMPLETIVE AUXILIARY)

TZ'OK = COMPLETIVE AUXILIARY

TZ'OK + SET A AFFIX =

TZ'IN

TZ'A

TZ'U

TZ'IN -O'ON

TZ'A -E'EX

TZ'U -O'OB

BIN / BINEL = TO GO (IRREGULAR VERB)

1	TZ'IN BIN	TZ'IN BINO'ON
	(I WENT)	(WE WENT) PL
2	TZ'A BIN	TZ'A BINE'EX
	(YOU WENT)	(YOU ALL WENT) PL
3	TZ'U BIN	TZ'U BINO'OB
	(HE / SHE WENT)	(THEY WENT)

IN ADDITION, THE ORIGINAL FORM OF THE
AUXILIARY CAN BE USED WITHOUT BLENDING
THE SET A AFFIXES:

TZ'OK IN BIN

TZ'OK A BIN

TZ'OK U BIN

TZ'OK IN BINO'ON

TZ'OK A BINE'EX

TZ'OK U BINO'OB

WITH VERBS THAT EXPRESS A STATE OF BEING
OR BECOMING:

-TAL (VERBAL ROOT ENDING)

SAASTAL = TO BECOME LIGHT (SAASIL = LIGHT)
[ADJECTIVE]

NOOKOYTAL = TO BECOME CLOUDY (NOOKOY =
OVERCAST [ADJECTIVE])

KULTAL = TO SIT DOWN (KULAL [VERB STEM])

WA'ALTAL = TO STAND UP (WA'AL [VERB STEM])

-TAL VERBS RECEIVE -CHAJ + SET B AFFIX WHEN THEY ARE CONJUGATED AS THE COMPLETIVE ASPECT OR PAST TENSE:

KUL | TAL

KULCHAJ + SET B AFFIX

KULCHAJEEN = I SAT (MYSELF) DOWN

KULTAL = TO SIT DOWN

1	KULCHAJEEN (I SAT DOWN)	KULCHAJO'ON (WE SAT DOWN) PL
2	KULCHAJEECH (YOU SAT DOWN)	KULCHAJE'EX (YOU ALL SAT DOWN) PL
3	KULCHAJI (HE / SHE SAT DOWN)	KULCHAJO'OB (THEY SAT DOWN) PL

The Future Tense: J- + SET A AFFIX... -E

(SUFFIXAL ENDING)

J- + SET A AFFIX... -E

JEN -E

JA' -E

JU' -E

JEK -E

JA' -E'EXI

JU' O'OBI

BIN / BINEL = TO GO (IRREGULAR VERB)

1	JEN BINE (I WILL GO)	JEK BINE (WE WILL GO) PL
2	JA' BINE (YOU WILL GO)	JA' BINE'EXI (YOU ALL WILL GO) PL
3	JU' BINE (HE, SHE, IT WILL GO)	JU' BINO'OBI (THEY WILL GO) PL

THERE ARE FOUR CLASSES OF VERBS IN THE YUCATEC LANGUAGE AND EACH OF THEM HAVE THE SAME RULES AS THE PREVIOUS EXAMPLES.

I)   JAAN<u>AL</u> = INTRANSITIVE
II)   JAANT<u>IK</u> = TRANSITIVE
III)   KUL<u>TAL</u> = STATE OF BEING OR BECOMING
IV)   BIN / BINEL = IRREGULAR

CLASS I

K'UCHUL (TO ARRIVE)

1	TIN K'UCHUL (I ARRIVE)	TANK K'UCHUL / TIN K'UCHULO'ON (WE ARRIVE) PL
2	TAN K'UCHUL (YOU ARRIVE)	TAN K'UCHULE'EX (YOU ALL ARRIVE) PL
3	TUN K'UCHUL (HE, SHE, IT ARRIVES)	TUN K'UCHULO'OB (THEY ARRIVE) PL

CLASS II

TZ'U'UTZ'IK (TO KISS)

1	TIN TZ'U'UTZ'IK (I KISS)	TANK TZ'U'UTZ'IK / TIN TZ'U'UTZ'IKO'ON (WE KISS) PL	
2	TAN TZ'U'UTZ'IK (YOU KISS)	TAN TZ'U'UTZ'IKE'EX (YOU ALL KISS) PL	
3	TUN TZ'U'UTZ'IK (HE, SHE, IT KISSES)	TUN TZ'U'UTZ'IKO'OB (THEY KISS) PL	

CLASS III

WA'ALTAL (TO STAND UP)

1	TIN WA'ALTAL (I STAND UP)	TANK WA'ALTAL / TIN WA'ALTALO'ON (WE STAND UP) PL
2	TAN WA'ALTAL (YOU STAND UP)	TAN WA'ALTALE'EX (YOU ALL STAND UP) PL
3	TUN WA'ALTAL (HE, SHE, IT STANDS UP)	TUN WA'ALTALO'OB (THEY STAND UP) PL

CLASS IV: IRREGULAR

BIN / BINEL (TO GO)

1	TIN BIN (I GO)	TANK BIN / TIN BINO'ON (WE GO) PL	
2	TAN BIN (YOU GO)	TAN BINE'EX (YOU ALL GO) PL	
3	TUN BIN (HE, SHE, IT GOES)	TUN BINO'OB (THEY GO) PL	

TAAL / TAALEL (TO COME)

1	TIN TAL (I COME)	TANK TAL / TIN TALO'ON (WE COME) PL	
2	TAN TAL (YOU COME)	TAN TALE'EX (YOU ALL COME) PL	
3	TUN TAL (HE, SHE, IT COMES)	TUN TALO'OB (THEY COME) PL	

TAAL / TAALEL (TO COME) WITH IRREGULAR PAST
TENSE WITH SET B AFFIX

1	TALEEN (I CAME)	TALO'ON (WE CAME) PL	
2	TALEECH (YOU CAME)	TALE'EX (YOU ALL CAME) PL	
3	TALI (HE, SHE, IT CAME)	TALO'OB (THEY CAME) PL	

CLASS III

-TAL VERB: STATE OF BEING OR BECOMING [CAN
BE USED WITH ADJECTIVES OR AN INTRANSITIVE
VERB STEM].

KULTAL (TO SIT DOWN) COMPLETIVE ASPECT -
CHAJ + SET B AFFIX

1	KULCHAJEEN (I SAT DOWN)	KULCHAJO'ON (WE SAT DOWN) PL	
2	KULCHAJEECH (YOU SAT DOWN)	KULCHAJE'EX (YOU SAT DOWN) PL	
3	KULCHAJI (HE, SHE, IT SAT DOWN)	KULCHAJO'OB (THEY SAT DOWN) PL	

49

MANY VERBAL FORMS NEED AN AUXILIARY TO CONVEY THEIR MEANING OR THUS EXPOUND ON THE VERBAL ROOT. THE FOLLOWING ARE SEVERAL AUXILIARIES USED WITHIN THE YUCATEC MAYA LANGUAGE AND EXAMPLES OF THEIR USE:

TAAN = USED TO CREATE PRESENT TENSE

(TIN, TAN, TUN, TANK, ETC.)

- TIN BIN = I AM GOING

K- = DEFAULT AUXILIARY; EXPRESSES HABITUAL TENDENCIES AND IS USED WHEN POSING A QUESTION

- ¿TU'UX KA BIN? = WHERE ARE YOU GOING?

J- = USED TO CREATE THE FUTURE TENSE

(JEN, JA', JU', JEK, ETC.)

- JEN BIN TI' IN WOTOCH = I WILL GO HOME

MA' = NEGATION; 'MA" IS AN AUXILIARY THAT MAKES VERBAL STRUCTURES NEGATIVE AND CAN BE BLENDED WITH SET A AFFIXES

(M'IN, MA', MU', ETC.)

- M'IN WOOJLI = I DON'T KNOW
- MA' TIN NA'ATIK TEECH = I DON'T UNDERSTAND YOU

TAAK = EXPRESSES DESIRE TO DO SOMETHING

- TAAK IN KANIK LE T'AANO' = I DESIRE TO LEARN THE WORDS

JO'OP = EXPRESSES THE BEGINNING OF AN ACTION

- JO'OP IN BEETIK = I AM BEGINNING TO DO IT
- JO'OP IN WILIK = I AM BEGINNING TO SEE IT

JOK' = EXPRESSES THE BEGINNING OF AN ACTION; COMMONLY USED IN QUINTANA ROO AND SURROUNDING AREAS.

- JOK' IN BEETIK = I AM BEGINNING TO DO IT
- JOK' IN WILIK = I AM BEGINNING TO SEE IT

K'ABEET = INDICATES THE NEED TO DO SOMETHING; IT IS NECESSARY THAT… / I NEED TO…

- K'ABEET IN MANIK LE WAAJOBO' = IT IS NECESSARY THAT I BUY THOSE TORTILLAS
- K'ABEET IN MEYAJ = IT IS NECESSARY THAT I WORK

YAN = INDICATES THE NEED TO DO SOMETHING; I HAVE TO…

- YAN IN BEETIK = I AM GOING TO DO IT / I HAVE TO DO IT
- YAN IN BINEL = I HAVE TO GO

YANJI = INDICATES THAT SOMETHING WAS NEEDED TO BE DONE [IN THE PAST]; I HAD TO...

- YANJI IN BEETIK = I HAD TO DO IT
- YANJI IN BINEL = I HAD TO GO

K'AAT = TO WANT

- ¿A K'AAT BINEL YETELEEN? = DO YOU WANT TO GO WITH ME?
- K'AAT IN BINEL TI' IN WOTOCH = I WANT TO GO HOME
- K'AAT IN JAANAL = I WANT TO EAT
- K'AAT IN BEETIK = I WANT TO DO IT
- ¿A K'AAT JAANAL? = DO YOU WANT TO EAT?
- K'AAT A JAANAL = YOU WANT TO EAT

PAATAL = TO BE ABLE

- ¿JU' PAATALE IN MANIK LE O'OCHO'? = CAN I BUY THAT FOOD?

PAAT = TO BE ABLE TO [SHORT FORM OF: PAATAL]

- PAAT IN WAANTIKEECH = I CAN HELP YOU
- PAAT IN BEETIK = I CAN DO IT
- ¿PAAT A WAANTIKEEN? = CAN YOU HELP ME?
- PAAT A BINEL = YOU CAN GO
- PAAT A TALEL YETELEEN = YOU CAN COME WITH ME
- PAAT IN TALEL YETELEECH = I CAN COME WITH YOU

MU' PATI = IT IS NOT POSSIBLE

- MU' PATI IN WAANTIKEECH = I CAN'T HELP YOU
- MU' PATI IN BEETIK = I CAN'T DO IT

CHABAL = TO BE ABLE TO; TO BE POSSIBLE

- ¿JU' CHABALE IN MENTIK POTO' WAYE? = WILL IT BE POSSIBLE TO TAKE A PHOTO HERE?
- ¿JU' CHABALE IN BINEL TI' IN WOTOCH? = WILL IT BE POSSIBLE TO GO HOME?

XI)   I to You and You to Me

The following table shows the Affixes used with the construction of verbs when there is a subject and a direct object in a verbal phrase, for example:

I LOVE YOU = KIN YAKUNTIKEECH

K (PRESENT TENSE) + **IN** (I) + **YAKUNTIK** (VERBAL ROOT) = TO LOVE + -**EECH** (YOU) [ALWAYS AT THE END OF THE VERBAL ROOT]

HERE IS A LIST OF ALL OF THE INFIX CONSTRUCTIONS:

I/YOU   IN (W-)...-EECH

I/HIM   IN (W-)...-I / TRANSITIVE VERB ENDING

I/YOU ALL   IN (W-)...-E'EX

I/THEM   IN (W-)...-O'OB

YOU/ME   A (W-)...-EEN

YOU/HIM   A (W-)...-I / TRANSITIVE VERB ENDING

YOU/US   A (W-)...-O'ON

YOU/THEM A (W-)...-O'OB

HE/ME   U (Y-)...-EEN

HE/YOU   U (Y-)...-EECH

HE/US   U (Y-)...-O'ON

HE/YOU ALL	U (Y-)...-E'EX
HE/THEM	U (Y-)...-O'OB
WE/YOU	K...-EECH
WE/HIM	K...-I / TRANSITIVE VERB ENDING
WE/YOU ALL	K...-E'EX
WE/THEM	K...-O'OB
YOU ALL / ME	A (W-)...-E'EX TEEN
YOU ALL / HIM	A (W-)...-E'EX TI'E / LEETI'
YOU ALL/ US	A (W-)...-E'EX TO'ON
YOU ALL / THEM	A (W-)...-E'EX TI'O'OB
THEY/ME	U (Y-)...O'OB TEEN
THEY/YOU	U (Y-)...-O'OB TEECH
THEY/US	U (Y-)...-O'OB TO'ON
THEY/YOU	U (Y-)...-O'OB TE'EX

XII) Verbal Adjectives and Passive Voice

The Verbal Adjective is not a common form in the Yucatec Maya Language, but there are examples of Verbal Adjectives in Yucatec that express the completive aspect. All in all, the Verbal Adjective is not as prominent in Yucatec as it is in other Mayan Languages.

KIIMIL = TO DIE

VERBS WITH -#L ENDINGS CAN TAKE THE ENDING -EN TO CREATE A PAST TENSE VERBAL ADJECTIVE.

EXAMPLE:

KIMEN = DEAD [ADJ]

-CAN BE USED AS AN ADJECTIVE IN THE SAME MANNER AS THEY ARE USED IN SPANISH WITH THE -ADO / -IDO FORMS.

-VERBAL ADJECTIVES IN YUCATEC CANNOT BE USED TO EXPRESS THE PERFECT ASPECT.

K'UCHUL = K'UCHEN = ARRIVED

JAANAL = JAANEN = EATEN

PASSIVE VOICE CAN BE COMPLETIVE OR INCOMPLETE. THERE ARE TWO SEPARATE SUFFIXES THAT CAN BE USED IN THE VERB STEM TO IMPLEMENT THE PASSIVE VOICE:

COMPLETIVE:

-AB + SET B AFFIX

TZ'ONIK = TO SHOOT SOMETHING [TRANSITIVE]

TZ'ON | IK

TZ'ONABEN = I WAS SHOT

JANTIK = TO EAT SOMETHING [TRANSITIVE]

JANT | IK

JANTABI = IT WAS EATEN

INCOMPLETE:

A) FUTURE AUXILIARY – (J-) WITH THE APPROPRIATE SET A AFFIX + -(#)LE = GOING TO BE DONE, WILL BE DONE (NOT DONE YET, BUT WILL BE) ['T' ROOT VERBS]

B) FUTURE AUXILIARY – (J-) WITH THE APPROPRIATE SET A AFFIX + -(#)LE = GOING TO BE DONE, WILL BE DONE (NOT DONE YET, BUT WILL BE) ['S' ROOT VERB]

FORMATION I 'T' ROOT VERBS

JANTIK = TO EAT SOMETHING [TRANSITIVE]

JANT | IK

JU' JANTALE = IT WILL BE EATEN

TZ'IIBTIK = TO WRITE SOMETHING [TRANSITIVE]

TZ'IIBT | IK

JU' TZ'IIBTILE = IT WILL BE WRITTEN

FORMATION II 'S' ROOT VERBS

KIINSIK = TO KILL SOMEONE (TRANSITIVE)

KIINS | IK

JEN KIINSILE = I WILL BE KILLED

E'ESIK = TO SHOW [TRANSITIVE VERB]

E'ES | IK

JEN E'ESILE = I WILL BE SHOWN

ADDITIONAL FORMULA:

BIN ... -(AL)AK- + SET BE AFFIX

'T' ROOT VERBS

TZ'IIBTIK = TO WRITE SOMETHING [TRANSITIVE VERB]

TZ'IIBT | IK

BIN TZ'IIBT(AL)AKI = IT IS GOING TO BE WRITTEN

'S' ROOT VERBS

KIINSIK

KIINS | IK

BIN KINS(AL)AKEN = I AM GOING TO BE KILLED

XIII) Negation

Negation is expressed with, 'Ma'...(i)' and is an auxiliary that can be blended with Set A Affixes. This blending with the negative auxiliary is very common in spoken Yucatec.

Negation of the Present

MA' (NOT) + IN (I) + K'AAT (WANT)

M'IN K'AAT (I DO NOT WANT)

IRREGULAR EXCEPTION: MU' PATI (TO NOT BE ABLE TO)

MA' (NOT) + U (3RD PERSON SING.) + PAATAL (CAN / IS POSSIBLE) + -I =

MU' PATI (I CANNOT / IT IS NOT POSSIBLE)

The past and future tenses are not blended due to the use of auxiliaries other than that of the negation:

MA' TZ'IN LUK'ULI = I DID NOT LEAVE

MA' TZ'OK IN LUK'ULI = I DID NOT LEAVE

MA' JEN LUK'ULI = I WILL NOT LEAVE

XIV) Commands

There are various types of commands (imperatives) in
the Yucatec Language; the following are examples of
each type:

TRANSITIVE VERBS:

TASIK = TO BRING

TAS | IK + TI'

¡TAS! = BRING!

¡TAS TEEN JUMP'EL CHEBA! = BRING ME A BEER!

JANTIK = TO EAT

JANT | IK

¡JANTE! = EAT!

TZ'IIK = TO GIVE (IRREGULAR STEM)

TZ'I (#) | IK

¡TZA' TEEN! = GIVE ME (IT)!

¡TZA' TEEN JUMP'EL CHEBA! = GIVE ME A BEER!

BEETIK = TO DO

BEET | IK

¡BEETE! = DO IT!

TZ'U'UTZ'IK = TO KISS

TZ'U'UTZ' | IK

¡TZ'U'UTZ'E TEEN! = KISS ME!

INTRANSITIVE VERBS RECEIVE THE -EN AFTER THE VERBAL ROOT

JAANAL = TO EAT

JAAN | AL

¡JAANEN! = EAT!

LUK'UL = TO LEAVE

LUK' | UL

¡LUK'EN! = GO AWAY! LEAVE!

ALL CONJUGATED VERBS IN THEIR IMPERATIVE VERBAL FORM CAN BE MADE PLURAL WITH -E'EX. MAKING A COMMAND PLURAL MEANS THAT YOU ARE SAYING THE COMMAND TO TWO OR MORE PEOPLE AND NOT JUST TO ONE PERSON.

¡LUK'EN! = ¡LUK'ENE'EX! = LEAVE! [MORE THAN ONE PERSON]

¡BEETE! = ¡BEETE'EX! = DO IT! [MORE THAN ONE PERSON]

IRREGULAR VERBS:

BIN / BINEL = TO GO

¡XEN! = GO! [TO ONE PERSON]

¡XENE'EX! = GO! [TO MORE THAN ONE PERSON]

TAAL / TAALEL = TO COME

¡KO'OTEN! = COME! [TO ONE PERSON]

¡KO'OTENE'EX! = COME! [TWO OR MORE PEOPLE]

¡KO'ONE'EX! = LET'S GO! [WE ALL GO]

XV)   Commands with negation

The form of commands with negation always has this construction:

MA' + IMPERATIVE CONJUGATION OF VERBALROOT

ALL OF THE SAME RULES APPLIED TO NON-NEGATED IMERATIVES REMAIN THE SAME ONLY THE NEGATIVE AUXILIARY 'MA" IS ADDED TO THE BEGINNING WITHOUT '-I' THAT USUALLY IS PRESENT WITH ALL OTHER TENSES.

TRANSITIVE VERBS CAN ALSO MAINTAIN THEIR VERBAL ROOT AND TRANSITIVE SUFFIX AND BE PRECEDED BY THE NEGATIVE AUXILIARY AND SET A AFFIXES.

EXAMPLES:

¡MA' JAANEN! = DON'T EAT!

¡MA' JAANENE'EX! = DON'T EAT! [PLURAL]

¡MA' JANTE! = DON'T EAT IT!

¡MA' JANTE'EX! = DON'T EAT IT! [PLURAL]

¡MA' BEETE! = DON'T DO IT!

¡MA' BEETE'EX! = DON'T DO IT! [PLURAL]

¡MA' A BEETIK! = DON'T DO IT!

¡MA' A BEETIKE'EX! = DON'T DO IT! [PLURAL]

¡MA' LUK'EN! = DON'T LEAVE!

¡MA' LUK'ENE'EX! = DON'T LEAVE! [PLURAL]

¡MA' XEN! = DON'T GO!

¡MA' XENE'EX! = DON'T GO! [PLURAL]

¡MA' KO'OTEN! = DON'T COME!

¡MA' KO'OTENE'EX!! = DON'T COME! [PLURAL]

XVI) Subjunctive

Subjunctive is not commonly used in Yucatec as it is in Spanish, but it is used occasionally; especially when the meaning that needs to be expressed is more of a polite tone, such as the: 'May the Lord Bless You.'

In general, it is a polite form to express that something may happen or that there is a need for something to happen, whether it is something wished for or desired.

In general, for transitive verbs:

SET A AFFIX + TRANSITIVE VERBAL ROOT + SET B AFFIX (DEFAULT -E SIMILAR TO IMPERATIVES, BUT WITH INCLUSION OF ALL SET B AFFIXES IF NEEDED).

U BEETE = HE / SHE MAY DO IT

A BEETE = YOU MAY DO IT

IN BEETE = I MAY DO IT

K BEETE = WE MAY DO IT

A BEETE'EX = YOU ALL MAY DO IT

U BEETE'O'OB = THEY MAY DO IT

WITH A OBJECT PRONOUN:

IN KINSEECH = I MAY KILL YOU

A JATZ'E LE PAALO' = YOU MAY HIT THE/THAT BOY

In general, for intransitive verbs:

VERBAL ROOT + (#)K [THE VOWEL IS DETERMINED BY THE VERBAL STEM] + WITH A SET B AFFIX ATTACHED EXCEPT IF IT IS 3RD PERSON SINGULAR.

KIIMIL = TO DIE

KIIM | IL

KIIMIK = HE / SHE MAY DIE

KIIMIKEECH = YOU MAY DIE

KIIMIKEEN = I MAY DIE

KIIMIKO'ON = WE MAY DIE

KIIMIKE'EX = YOU ALL MAY DIE

KIIMIKO'OB = THEY MAY DIE

IRREGULAR: BIN /BINEL = XI'IK [MAY GO]

XVII) Oneself = (#) + BA

(#) + BA is used like 'a mi mismo, a ti mismo, a si mismo, etc.' in Spanish. The equivalent in English would be 'myself, yourself, his self, etc.' Or simply 'oneself' and of course, this form changes when a personal possessive prefix is used:

Oneself = (#) + BA

1	IN BA (myself)	K BA (ourselves)
2	A BA (yourself	*A BA (yourselves)
3	U BA (hisself, herself, itself)	*U BA (themselves)

*THESE TWO FORMS ARE TO BE USED THE SAME AS THEIR SINGULAR COUNTERPARTS, BUT ONLY WITH CONSTRUCTIONS OF A PLURAL VERBAL FORM.

Examples:

¡PEEK [A BA]! (Move [yourself]!) *Imperative*

¡E'ESE A BA! (Show [yourself]!) *Imperative*

TZ'U WA'AK U BA JOOL LE K'IINO' = HE STOOD ALL
DAY LONG

¡WA'AK A BA WAYE' YETEL MA' PEEK A BA! =
STAND HERE AND DON'T MOVE!

XVIII)   Adverbs, Conjunctions and Prepositions

Adverbs, Conjunctions and Prepositions are used very simply in Yucatec as they are in most Mayan Languages; only Prepositions may include an affix to indicate the subject's position or location. The following is a list of Adverbs, Conjunctions and Prepositions in the Yucatec Maya Language.

Format – Yucatec Maya = Spanish / English

*Spanish is included for quick referencing purposes

AASTA = HASTA / UNTIL

AK' AB = NOCHE / NIGHT

ASAB = CASI / ALMOST

BE'OORA' = AHORA / NOW

BE'OORITA' = AHORITA / RIGHT NOW

BEJLA' AK = HOY; ANTERIORMENTE / TODAY; BEFORE

BEJLA' E' = HOY / TODAY

BEYA' = ASÍ / LIKE THIS

BEYO' = ASÍ / LIKE THAT

CHAANBEEL = LENTO, DESPACIO / SLOW, SLOWLY

CHUUMUK = ENTRE; EN MEDIO DE / BETWEEN, AMONG, IN THE MIDDLE OF

EET = IGUAL; JUNTO; PAREJO / EQUAL; TOGETHER; PAIR

ICHIL = ADENTRO DE; DENTRO DE; EN / WITHIN; INSIDE; IN

JAAJ = ES VERDAD(ERO) / IT'S TRUE, IS IT TRUE...?

JAAL (-JAAL) [IN JAAL, A JAAL, U JAAL, ETC.] = LADO / SIDE (OF)

JACH = MUCH; MUY / MUCH; VERY

JACH YA'AB [ADJ.] = MUCHO; MUCHOS / MANY

JATZKAB K'IIN = MADRUGADA; MAÑANITA / IN THE MORNING, EARLY MORNING

JE'ELA' = AQUÍ ESTÁ / HERE IT IS

JE'ELO' = ALLÁ ESTÁ / THERE IT IS

JO'OLJEYAK = AYER / YESTERDAY

JOOL = TODO(A) / ALL (OF)

JUMP'IIT = POCO, POQUITO / A LITTLE, A LITTLE BIT

K'AABET = TENER QUE / TO HAVE TO

KA'AJ [CONJ.] = CUANDO / WHEN

KA'AJ [CONJ.] = QUE / THAT

KA'AJ = OTRA VEZ; YA; OTRO / AGAIN, STILL, ALREADY, OTHER

KA'AKA'TE' = DESPUÉS / AFTER(WARDS)

KAABAL = ABAJO, DEBAJO DE... / UNDER..., BENEATH...

KEX = AUNQUE / ALTHOUGH

LAAJ = TODO(A) / ALL (OF)

LAAYLI'E' = SIEMPRE / ALWAYS

LE'BEETIK = POR ESO / FOR THAT

MA'A TEECH = NUNCA / NEVER

MIX BIK'IN = NUNCA / NEVER

MIX MAAK = NADIE / NO ONE

MIXBA'AL = NADA / NOTHING

NAATZ' = CERCA DE, ALREDEDOR DE / NEAR, CLOSE TO, AROUND, IN THE VICINITY OF

PERO = PERO / BUT

SAAM = YA / ALREADY

SAAMAL = MAÑANA / TOMORROW

SANSAAMAL = DIARIAMENTE; DIARIO / DAILY

SEEB = RÁPIDO / FAST

SEEBAK [ADJ.] = RÁPIDO / FAST

TA'AYTAK = YA MERO; CASI / ALMOST; ALREADY

TAANIL = ENFRENTE, ADELANTE DE… / IN FRONT OF….

TANILI = YA; DESDE; ENTONCES / ALREADY

TI' = A; EN / TO; IN; AT; ON

TI' AK'AB = DE NOCHE, EN LA NOCHE / AT NIGHT, IN THE NIGHT

TI' KA'AN = ARRIBA; EN EL CIELO / UP; IN THE SKY

TI' TZEEL = AL LADO DE / AT THE SIDE OF

TU PAACH = ATRÁS DE, DETRÁS DE / BEHIND, AT THE BACK OF, NEAR, OVER, ABOUT, FOR, IN ORDER TO

TULAAKAL = TODO(A) / ALL (OF)

TUMEN = PORQUE / BECAUSE

TZEEL (-TZEEL) [IN TZEEL, A TZEEL, U TZEEL, ETC.] = LADO / SIDE (OF)

WAAJ = O / OR

WAAJ BA'AX = ALGO; ALGUNO / SOMETHING; SOME

WAAJ MAAX = ALGUIEN; ALGUNO / SOMEONE; SOME

WAAJ TU'UX = ADONDE / SOMEWHERE

XAN = ADÉMAS, TAMBIÉN / IN ADDITION, ALSO

YA'AB = MUCHO / MUCH

YAAN = TENER QUE / TO HAVE TO

YAANAL = ABAJO, DEBAJO DE... / UNDER..., BENEATH...

YEETEL = CON; JUNTO / TOGETHER; WITH

Yucatec Maya Phrasebook

* The order of the phrases are as follows: Spanish / English – Yucatec Maya

*Remember that the 'j' is pronounced like in Spanish like a rough 'h'

I)   Hello's and Goodbye's

¡HOLA! / HELLO! = ¡OOLA!

¿QUÉ TAL? ¿QUÉ ONDA? / WHAT'S UP? WHAT'S GOING ON? = ¿TU'UX KA BIN? [LITERALLY: WHERE ARE YOU GOING?]

¿CÓMO ESTÁS? ¿CÓMO ESTÁN USTEDES? / HOW ARE YOU? = ¿B'IX A BEEL? [SINGULAR] … ¿B'IX A BEELE'EX? [PLURAL]

¿CÓMO ESTÁS? ¿CÓMO ESTÁN USTEDES? / HOW ARE YOU? =

¿B'IX YAANIKEECH? ¿B'IX YAANILEECH? [SINGULAR]

¿B'IX YAANIKE'EX? ¿B'IX YAANILE'EX? [PLURAL]

¿CÓMO ESTÁS? / HOW ARE YOU? = ¿BA'AX KA WA'ALIK? [LITERALLY: WHAT DO YOU SAY?]

¡ADIÓS! / GOODBYE! = ¡TAK SAAMAL!

¡NOS VEMOS! / SEE YOU AGAIN SOON! = ¡TAK SAAMAL!

¡ADIÓS! / BYE! = ¡KA XI'IK TEECH UTZIIL!

¡BUENA SUERTE! / GOOD LUCK! MAY IT GO WELL WITH YOU! = ¡KA XI'IK TEECH JATZ'UTZIIL!

¡DIOS TE PROTEJA! / MAY GOD PROTECT YOU! = ¡KA'AJ DYOS KALAANTEECH!

II) Basic phrases of conversation

SÍ / YES = JAAJ

NO / NO = MA'

¿CÓMO ESTÁS? ¿CÓMO ESTÁN USTEDES? / HOW ARE YOU? = ¿B'IX A BEEL? [SINGULAR] ¿B'IX A BEELE'EX? [PLURAL]

¡ESTOY BIEN, GRACIAS! / I'M WELL, THANK YOU = MA'ALOB / UTZ, JACH DYOS BO'OTIK TEECH / DYOS BO'OTIK TEECH

VARIANTS:

YU'UM BO'OTIK TEECH / JACH YUUM BO'OTIK TEECH

¿Y TÚ? ¿CÓMO ESTÁS? /AND YOU? HOW ARE YOU? = ¿KUX TEECH? ¿B'IX A BEEL?

ESTOY BIEN / I AM WELL = (JACH) MA'ALOB

DE NADA / YOU'RE WELCOME = MA', DYOS BO'OTIK TEECH [RESPONSE TO THANK YOU]

VARIANTS:

MA', YUUM BO'OTIK TEECH / MA', JACH YUUM BO'OTIK TEECH

ESTÁ BIEN / ALL IS WELL = MA'ALOB

¿CÓMO TE LLAMAS? / WHAT'S YOUR NAME? =
¿B'IX A K'ABA'? ¿BA'AX A K'ABA'?

ME LLAMO... / MY NAME IS... = IN K'ABA'E...

NO TE CONOZCO / I DON'T KNOW YOU = MA' TIN
KAJOOLTIKEECH

TÚ NO ME CONOCES / YOU DON'T KNOW ME =
MA' TAN KAJOOLTIKEECH

¿DE DÓNDE ERES? / WHERE ARE YOU FROM? =
¿TU'UX A TAAL?

¿DE DÓNDE ERES? / WHERE ARE YOU FROM? =
¿TU'UX A KAAJAL?

SOY DE LOS ESTADOS UNIDOS / I'M FROM THE
UNITED STATES = LUK'EN LOS ESTADOS UNIDOS

¿CUÁNTOS AÑOS TIENES? / HOW OLD ARE YOU? =
¿JAYP'EL AANYOS YAAN TEECH? ¿JAYP'EL A
JA'ABIIL?

*TENGO...AÑOS / I AM...YEARS OLD =

YAAN TEEN...JA'ABIIL

JUN = 1

KA'A =2

OOX = 3

KAN = 4

JO' = 5

WAAK = 6

UK = 7

WAXAK = 8

BOLON = 9

LAJUN = 10

BULUK = 11

LAJKA'A = 12

OOX LAJUN = 13

KAN LAJUN = 14

JO' LAJUN = 15

WAK LAJUN = 16

UK LAJUN = 17

WAXAK LAJUN = 18

BOLON LAJUN = 19

JUN K'AAL = 20

JUN K'AAL JUN = 21

JUN K'AAL KA'A = 22

JUN K'AAL OOX = 23

JUN K'AAL KAN = 24

JUN K'AAL JO' = 25

JUN K'AAL WAK = 26

JUN K'AAL UK = 27

JUN K'AAL WAXAK = 28

JUN K'AAL BOLON = 29

KA' K'AAL = 40

OOX K'AAL = 60

KAN K'AAL = 80

JO' K'AAL = 100

POR FAVOR, DIME ESO EN ESPAÑOL / PLEASE, TELL ME THAT IN SPANISH = ¡A'ANE TEEN TI' LE KAXLANT'AANO'!

¿HABLAS YUCATECO? / DO YOU SPEAK YUCATEC? = ¿KA T'AANIK LE MAAYAT'AANO'?

YO HABLO YUCATECO / I SPEAK YUCATEC = KIN T'AANIK LE MAAYAT'AANO'

NO HABLO YUCATECO / I DON'T SPEAK YUCATEC = MA' TEN T'ANIK LE MAAYAT'AANO'

POR FAVOR, HABLA LENTO / PLEASE SPEAK SLOWLY = ¡T'ANE CHAAMBEEL!

POR FAVOR, DIGÁME ESO OTRA VEZ / TELL ME THAT AGAIN PLEASE = ¡A'ANE TEEN KA'AJ!

¿QUÉ QUIERES QUE YO DIGA? / WHAT DO YOU WANT ME TO SAY? = ¿BA'AX A K'AAT KA'AJ TEN WA'ALIK?

TÚ HABLAS DEMASIADO RÁPIDO / YOU TALK TOO FAST = KA T'AAN JACH SEEB

LO SIENTO / I'M SORRY = MA' TAALI'TEENI'

NO ENTIENDO / I DON'T UNDERSTAND = MA' TIN NA'ATIK TEECH

¿TÚ SABES? / DO YOU KNOW? = ¿M'A WOJLI?

NO, NO SE / NO, I DON'T KNOW = MA', M'IN WOJLI

NO QUIERO SABER LO QUE PASÓ / I DON'T WANT TO KNOW WHAT HAPPENED = M'IN K'AAT IN WOJEL KA'AJ TZ'OK U YUUCHUL

NO QUIERO SABER / I DON'T WANT TO KNOW =
M'IN K'AAT IN WOJEL

¡PERDÓNAME! / EXCUSE ME! = ¡PA'ATIKI'!

¡TEN PRISA! ¡TENGA PRISA! ¡APÚRATE! / HURRY!
BE QUICK! = ¡SEEKUNTE!

¡VETE! ¡VAYASE! ¡VAYANSE! / GO! = ¡XEN! [TO ONE
PERSON] ¡XENE'EX! [TO TWO OR MORE PERSONS]

¡VEN ACÁ! ¡VENGA ACÁ! ¡VENGAN ACÁ! / COME
HERE! = ¡KO'OTEN WAYE'! [TO ONE PERSON]
¡KO'OTENE'EX WAYE'! [TO TWO OR MORE
PERSONS]

¿CUÁNDO TU LLEGASTE AQUÍ? / WHEN DID YOU
ARRIVE HERE? = ¿BA'AX K'IIN K'UCHEECH WAYE'?

YO LLEGUÉ AQUÍ AYER / I ARRIVED HERE
YESTERDAY = JO'OLJEYAK K'UCHEEN WAYE'

*THE MAJORITY OF YUCATEC MAYA WORK AS FARMERS OR, IN GENERAL, WITH GROWING CROPS; WHICH NOT ONLY FEEDS THEIR FAMILIES, BUT ALSO MAY PROVIDE EXCESS THAT THEY CAN SELL IN LOCAL MARKETS FOR PROFIT

¿EN QUÉ TÚ TRABAJAS? / WHAT KIND OF WORK DO YOU DO? = ¿MAAKALMAAK MEYAJ KA BEETIK?

SOY UN... / I WORK AS A... = IN MEYAJ...

SOY UN MILPERO / I AM A FARMER = KOOLNAALEEN / KINMEYAJ TI' KOOL

- JEN JOCHIKI = LO COSECHARÉ / I WILL HARVEST IT
- TEN BIN TZ'ON = VOY PARA CAZAR / I AM GOING HUNTING
- TEN BIN XOTIK SI' = VOY PARA CORTAR LEÑA / I AM GOING TO CUT FIREWOOD
- JEN BEETIKI SI' = VOY A HACER LA LEÑA / I WILL SEARCH FOR FIREWOOD

¿ADÓNDE VAS? / WHERE ARE YOU GOING? = ¿TU'UX KA BIN?

¿ADÓNDE FUÍSTE? / WHERE DID YOU GO? = ¿TU'UX BIINEECH?

¿ADÓNDE VAN USTEDES? / WHERE ARE YOU ALL GOING? = ¿TU'UX KA BINE'EX?

¿ADÓNDE FUERON USTEDES? / WHERE DID YOU ALL GO? = ¿TU'UX BIINE'EX?

¿CON QUIÉN FUÍSTE TÚ? / WHO DID YOU GO WITH? = ¿MAAX YETEL BIINEECH?

TENGO QUE IR / I HAVE TO GO = YAAN IN BINEL

TENGO QUE TRABAJAR / I HAVE TO WORK = YAAN IN MEYAJ

TENGO QUE SALIR / I HAVE TO LEAVE = YAAN IN LUK'UL

TENGO QUE HACERLO / I HAVE TO DO IT = YAAN IN BEETIK

VOY A REGRESAR / I WILL RETURN = YAAN IN SUUT

VOY A REGRESAR OTRA VEZ / I WILL RETURN AGAIN = YAAN IN SUUT KA'AJ

VOY A REGRESAR MAÑANA / I WILL RETURN TOMORROW = YAAN IN SUUT SAAMAL

VOY A REGRESAR EN EL PRÓXIMO AÑO / I WILL RETURN NEXT YEAR = JEN SUUTE TI' LAAK' JA'ABIIL

VAMOS A REGRESAR EN EL PRÓXIMO AÑO / WE WILL RETURN NEXT YEAR = JEK SUUTE TI' LAAK' JA'ABIIL

¿DÓNDE ESTÁ EL BANCO? / WHERE IS THE BANK? = ¿TU'UX YAAN LE BAANKO?

LLÉVAME AL BANCO / TAKE ME TO THE BANK = BIISE TEEN TI' BAANKO!

NECESITO CAMBIAR UN POCO DINERO / I NEED TO EXCHANGE SOME MONEY = YAAN IN K'EXIK JUMP'IIT TAAK'IN

QUIERO CAMBIAR [CANJEAR] DINERO / I WANT TO EXCHANGE MONEY = K'AAT IN K'EXIK LE TAAK'INA'

NO TENGO PESOS MEXICANOS / I DON'T HAVE MEXICAN PESOS = MA' YAANI' TEEN PEESOS

QUIERO PESOS MEXICANOS / I WANT MEXICAN PESOS = IN K'AAT PEESOS

¿DÓNDE ESTÁ EL MERCADO [TIENDA]? / WHERE IS THE MARKET [STORE]? = ¿TU'UX YAAN MERKAADO?

LLÉVAME AL MERCADO / TAKE ME TO THE MARKET = BIISE TEEN TI' MERKAADO

NECESITO COMPRAR COMIDA / I NEED TO BUY FOOD = YAAN IN MANIK JAANAL

NECESITO COMPRAR FRUTA / I NEED TO BUY FRUIT = YAAN IN MANIK CH'UJUK

¿QUÉ ES ESO? ¿QUÉ ES ESTO? / WHAT IS THAT? WHAT IS THIS? WHAT IS IT? = ¿BA'AXI?

¿CUÁNTO CUESTA? / HOW MUCH DOES IT [THAT] COST? = ¿BAJUUX U TOJOL?

¿CUÁNTO TE DEBO? / HOW MUCH DO I OWE YOU? = ¿BAJUUX K'AABET IN TZ'IIKEECH?

NO QUIERO COMPRAR ESTO/ I DON'T WANT TO BUY THIS = MA' M'IN K'AAT MANIK LELO'

SÍ, LO QUIERO COMPRAR / YES, I WANT TO BUY IT = JAAJ, K'AAT IN MANIK LELO'

LO SIENTO, NO LO PUEDO COMPRAR / I'M SORRY, I CAN'T BUY IT = MA' TAALI'TEENI', M'IN K'AAT IN MANIK LELO'

¿HAY ALGO MÁS BARATO? / IS THERE SOMETHING A LOT CHEAPER? = ¿YAAN JUMP'EL BA'AL MAAS MA' KO'OJI?

NO TENGO MUCHO DINERO / I DON'T HAVE MUCH MONEY = MA' YAANI TEEN JACH YA'AB TAAK'IN

SI YO TUVIERA DINERO SUFICIENTE, YO LO COMPRARÍA / IF I HAD SUFFICIENT MONEY, I WOULD BUY IT = WAAJ YAANJI TEEN JACH YA'AB TAAK'IN, KU PAAJTAL IN MANIK LELO'

¿TE GUSTA? / DO YOU LIKE IT? = ¿UTZ TAN WICH?

ME GUSTA / I LIKE IT = UTZ TIN WICH

NO, NO ME GUSTA / NO, I DON'T LIKE IT = MA', MA' UTZ TIN WICH

¿DÓNDE ESTÁ UNA TIENDA QUE VENDE...? / WHERE IS THERE A STORE THAT SELLS...? = ¿TU'UX YAAN JUMP'EL MERKAADO KA'AJ KU KONIK...?

NOOK' = ROPA / CLOTHING

KAMIISA = PLAYERA, CAMISA / SHIRT, T-SHIRTS

EEX = PANTALONES / PANTS

XANAB = ZAPATOS / SHOES

O'OCH = COMIDA / FOOD

JAANAL = COMIDA / FOOD

NOOK' = TELA; TEJIDO / BLANKETS; WEAVED FABRICS

JU'UNO'OB = LIBROS / BOOKS

SIIJBILO'OB = REGALOS / GIFTS

P'OKO'OB = SOMBREROS / HATS

WAAJO'OB = TORTILLAS / TORTILLAS

KOOKA = COCA COLA

QUIERO ATRÁVESAR EL RÍO / I WANT TO CROSS THE RIVER = K'AAT IN K'AATIK LE BEKANA'

QUEREMOS ATRÁVESAR EL RÍO / WE WANT TO CROSS THE RIVER = K'AAT IN K'AATIKO'ON LE BEKANA'

¿CUÁNTO CUESTA PARA LLEVARNOS A...? / HOW MUCH DOES IT COST TO TAKE US TO...? = ¿BAJUUX U TOJOL WAAJ TAN BISIKO'ON TI'...?

TODOS MIS COMPAÑEROS QUIEREN IR AL MERCADO PARA COMPRAR / VER LAS COSAS ALLÁ / ALL OF MY FRIENDS WANT TO GO TO THE MARKET TO BUY / SEE THE THINGS THERE =

TULAAKAL IN WAMIIGOJO'OB K'AAT U BINO'OB TI' MERKAADO MANIK / YILIK LE BA'ALO'OBO' TE'ELO'

TENGO HAMBRE / I'M HUNGRY = WI'IJEEN

TENGO SED / I'M THIRSTY = UK'AJEEN

VAMOS A BUSCAR COMIDA / LET'S LOOK FOR FOOD = JEK KAXTIKE O'OCH

NECESITO USAR EL BAÑO / I NEED TO USE THE RESTROOM = YAAN IN BINEL TI' BAANYO

¿DÓNDE ESTÁ EL BAÑO? / WHERE IS THE BATHROOM? = ¿TU'UX YAAN LE BAANYO'O'?

DÁME UN CAFÉ, POR FAVOR / GIVE ME A COFFEE, PLEASE = TZ'A TEEN JUMP'EL BOXJA'

TÚ ERES MUY HERMOSO(A) / GUAPO(A) / YOU ARE VERY BEAUTIFUL /HANDSOME = JATZ'UTZEECH / KI'ICHPANEECH

TÚ TIENE UNA CARA MUY LINDA / YOU HAVE A VERY CUTE FACE = YAAN TEECH JUMP'EL JATZ'UTZ IICH

¿PUEDO SACAR UNA FOTO? / I CAN TAKE A PHOTO? = ¿JU' CHABALE IN MENTIK JUMP'EL POTO?

¿PUEDO TOMAR UNA FOTO AQUÍ O NO? / CAN I TAKE A PHOTO HERE OR NO? = ¿KU PAAJTAL IN MENTIK POTO WAYE' WAAJ MA'?

¿HAY UN HOTEL AQUÍ? / IS THERE A HOTEL HERE? = ¿YAAN JUMP'EL OOTEL WAYE'?

LLÉVAME AL HOTEL / TAKE ME TO THE HOTEL = BISE TEEN TI' OOTEL

¿HAY UN CUARTO DISPONIBLE EN CUAL PUEDO QUEDARME / DORMIR? / IS THERE A ROOM AVAILABLE IN WHICH I CAN STAY / SLEEP? =

¿YAAN JUMP'EL BAANDA KA'AJ JU' PAAJTAL IN P'AATAL / IN WENEL?

¿CUÁNTAS NOCHES QUIERES QUEDARTE? / HOW MANY NIGHTS DO YOU WANT TO STAY? = ¿BAJUUX AK'ABO'OB A K'AAT P'AATAL WAYE'?

QUIERO QUEDARME AQUÍ POR UNO / DOS / TRES NOCHES / I WANT TO STAY HERE FOR ONE / TWO / THREE NIGHTS = K'AAT IN P'AATAL WAYE' JUMP'EL AK'AB / KA'AP'EL AK'ABO'OB / OOXP'EL AK'ABO'OB

¿CUÁNTO CUESTA EL CUARTO? / HOW MUCH DOES THE ROOM COST? = ¿BAJUUX U TOJOL LE BAANDA'A?

¿PUEDO VER EL CUARTO? / CAN I SEE THE ROOM? = ¿JU' PAAJTAL IN WILIK LA BAANDA'O'?

NO ME GUSTA / I DON'T LIKE IT = MA' UTZ TIN WICH

ME GUSTA, QUIERO EL CUARTO / I LIKE IT, I'LL TAKE IT = UTZ TIN WICH, IN K' AAT LE BAANDA' A'

EL CUARTO ES SUCIO, QUIERO OTRO / THE ROOM IS DIRTY, I WANT A DIFFERENT ONE = LE BAANDA' A' JACH EEK', IN K' AAT LAAK' BAANDA

TODAS LAS SÁBANAS SON SUCIAS / ALL OF THE SHEETS ARE DIRTY = TULAAKAL LE SABANA'O'OBO' JACH EEK'

¿DURMIERON USTEDES BIEN? / DID YOU ALL SLEEP WELL? = ¿TZ'OK A WENELE'EX MA'ALOB?

NO DORMÍ BIEN / I DID NOT SLEEP WELL = MA' TZ'OK IN WENELI

¿PORQUÉ? / WHY? = ¿BA'AXTEN...?

HABÍA DEMASIADO MUCHO RUÍDO / THERE WAS TOO MUCH NOISE = YAAN YA'AB JUUM WAYE'

QUIERO SALIR / I WANT TO LEAVE = K'AAT IN LUK'UL

VAMOS A BUSCAR OTRO HOTEL / LET'S LOOK FOR ANOTHER HOTEL = YAAN IN KAXTIKO'ON LAAK' OOTEL

¿QUIERES IR CONMIGO? / DO YOU WANT TO GO WITH ME? = ¿A K'AAT BINEL YETELEEN?

NO, NO PUEDO IR CONTIGO / NO, I CANNOT GO WITH YOU = MA', MU' PATI IN BINEL YETELEECH

NO, NO QUIERO IR CONTIGO / NO, I DO NOT WANT TO GO WITH YOU = MA', M'IN K'AAT BINEL YETELEECH

¿TE PUEDO AYUDAR? / CAN I HELP YOU? = ¿KU PAAJTAL IN WAANTIKEECH?

NO TE PUEDO AYUDAR / I CANNOT HELP YOU = MU' PAATI IN WAANTIKEECH

QUIERO QUE ME AYUDES / I WANT YOU TO HELP ME = IN K'AAT KA'AJ TAN WAANTIKEEN

SI YO TUVIERA DINERO, TE AYUDARÍA / IF I HAD MONEY, I WOULD HELP YOU = WAAJ YAANJI TEEN YA'AB TAAK'IN, JU' PAAJTAL IN WAANTIKEECH

SI YO TUVIERA DINERO, ME IRÍA / IF I HAD MONEY, I WOULD LEAVE = WAAJ YAANJI TEEN YA'AB TAAK'IN, JEN LUK'ULE

¿PORQUÉ ME QUIERES AYUDAR? / WHY DO YOU WANT TO HELP ME? = ¿BA'AXTEN A K'AAT A WAANTIKEEN?

¿ESTO ES TUYO? / IS THIS YOURS? = ¿A TI'AL LELA'?

ESTO NO ES TUYO / THIS IS NOT YOURS = MA'ATI'AAL LELA'

NO ES MÍO / IT IS NOT MINE = M'IN TI'AAL LELO'

SÍ, ES MÍO / YES, IT IS MINE = JAAJ, IN TI'AAL LELO'

OJALÁ TENGAS UN BUEN DÍA / I HOPE THAT YOU HAVE A GOOD DAY = KA'AJ YAAN TEECH JUMP'EL UTZ K'IIN

OJALÁ PUEDAS VENIR / HOPEFULLY YOU CAN COME = KA'AJ TAALAK

OJALÁ PUEDA YO ENCONTRARLO / I HOPE THAT I CAN FIND IT = KA'AJ A KAXTE

OJALÁ NO LLUEVA HOY / HOPEFULLY IT DOES NOT RAIN TODAY = KA'AJ MU' BEETE CHAAK BEJLA'E'

¿DÓNDE ESTÁ LA IGLESIA? / WHERE IS THE CHURCH? = ¿TU'UX YAAN YOTOCH DYOS?

LLÉVAME A LA IGLESIA / TAKE ME TO THE CHURCH = BIISE TEEN TI' YOTOCH DYOS

¿DÓNDE ESTÁ TU CASA? / WHERE IS YOUR HOME? = ¿TU'UX A NAJIIL?

DIOS TE BENDIGA / GOD BLESS YOU = KA'AJ DYOS KU BENDISYONTIKEECH

DIOS LOS BENDIGA / GOD BLESS YOU ALL = KA'AJ DYOS KU BENDISYONTIKE'EX

VAMOS A ORAR POR LA COMIDA / WE SHALL PRAY FOR OUR FOOD = JEK BO'OTIKE DYOS UTI'AL LE O'OCHA'

VAMOS A ORARLE A DIOS Y DARLE GRACIAS / LET'S PRAY TO GOD AND GIVE THANKS = JEK BO'OTIKE DYOS

DIOS ES MUY BUENO / GOD IS GOOD; GOD IS GREAT = DYOS JACH UTZ

DIOS NOS HA BENDECIDO CON OTRO DÍA / GOD HAS BLESSED US WITH ANOTHER DAY = DYOS U TZ'IIKO'ON UTZIIL YETEL TUUMBEN K'IIN

TE AMO / I LOVE YOU = KIN YAKUNTIKEECH

¿ME AMAS? / DO YOU LOVE ME? = ¿KA' YAKUNTIKEEN?

TE QUIERO BESAR / I WANT TO KISS YOU = K'AAT IN TZ'U'UTZ'IKEECH

TE QUIERO ABRAZAR / I WANT TO HUG YOU = K'AAT IN MEEK'IKEECH

TE QUIERO ENVOLVER BIEN EN MIS BRAZOS / I WANT TO WRAP YOU IN MY ARMS = K'AAT IN TO'IKEECH TI' IN K'ABO'OB

TE EXTRAÑARÉ MUCHO / I WILL MISS YOU VERY MUCH = YAAN TEEN XMA'EECH JACH YA'AB

NUNCA TE VOY A OLVIDAR / I WILL NEVER FORGET YOU = MIX B'IKIN KIN TU'UBSIKEECH

SOLO QUIERO QUEDARME A TU LADO / I ONLY WANT TO STAY AT YOUR SIDE = TAAK IN P'AATAL TI' A TZEEL

III)   COMMON COMMANDS [Imperatives]:

¡VETE! ¡VAYASE! ¡VAYANSE! / GO! = ¡XEN! [TO ONE PERSON] ¡XENE'EX! [TO TWO OR MORE PERSONS]

¡VEN ACÁ! ¡VENGA ACÁ! ¡VENGAN ACÁ! / COME HERE! = ¡KO'OTEN WAYE'! [TO ONE PERSON] ¡KO'OTENE'EX WAYE'! [TO TWO OR MORE PERSONS]

¡VEN CONMIGO! ¡VENGA CONMIGO! ¡VENGAN CONMIGO! / COME WITH ME! = ¡KO'OTEN YETELEEN! [TO ONE PERSON] ¡KO'OTENE'EX YETELEEN! [TO TWO OR MORE PERSONS]

¡LARGATE DE AQUÍ! / GET OUT OF HERE! LEAVE ME IN PEACE! = XEN TE'ELO'!

¡VAMOS! ¡VAYAMOS! / LET'S GO! = ¡KO'ONE'EX!

¡VAMOS A COMER! / LET'S EAT! = ¡JEK JAANALE!

¡TRABAJEMOS! / LET'S WORK! = ¡JEK MEYAJE!

¡VÁYASE A TRABAJAR! / GO TO WORK! = ¡MEYAJ! [SING.] ¡MEYAJE'EX! [PLURAL]

¡HÁGAMOSLO! / LET'S DO IT! = ¡JEK BEETIKE!

¡VÁYASE A HACERLO! / GO DO TI! = ¡BEETE! [SING] ¡BEETE'EX! [PLURAL]

¡HÁGALO! / DO IT! = BEETE!

¡NO LO HAGAS! / DON'T DO IT! = ¡MA' A BEETIK!

HÁGAME UN FAVOR / DO ME A FAVOR, PLEASE = BEETE TEEN JUMP'EL UTZIIL

¡VAMOS A HACERLO! / LET'S DO IT! = ¡JEK BEETIKE!

¡VAMOS A HACER LA LEÑA! / LET'S COLLECT FIRE WOOD! = ¡JEK BEETIKE SI'!

¡VAMOS A BAILAR! / LET'S DANCE! = ¡JEK OK'OTE!

¡DÁMELO! / GIVE ME IT! = ¡TZ'AA TEEN!

DAME DOS CERVEZAS, POR FAVOR / GIVE ME TWO BEERS, PLEASE = TZ'AA TEEN KA'AP'EL CHEBA'O'OB

DAME UNA BOTELLA DE AGUA / UNA COCA COLA / GIVE ME A BOTTLE OF WATER / A COCA COLA = TZ'AA TEEN JUMP'EL SIIS JA' / JUMP'EL KOOKA

¡BEBA! / DRINK! = ¡UK'EN!

¡BEBA AGUA! / DRINK WATER! = ¡UK'EN JA!

¡ÉNTRATE! ¡ÉNTRESE! ¡ÉNTRENSE! / ENTER! COME IN! = ¡OOKEN! [SING] ¡OOKENE'EX! [PLURAL]

¡AGUÁRDAME AQUÍ! / WAIT FOR ME HERE! = ¡PA'ATE WAYE'!

LLÉVAME AL MERCADO / TAKE ME TO THE MARKET = BIISE TEEN TI' MERKAADO

IV)   EMERGENCY PHRASES:

¡AYÚDAME! ¡AYUDENME! / HELP ME! = ¡A'ANTE!
[TO ONE PERSON] ¡A'ANTE'EX! [TWO OR MORE
PERSONS]

¡NO TE CAÍGAS! / DON'T FALL! = ¡MA' LUUBEN!

¡NO ME MOLESTES! ¡NO ME CHINGUES! / DON'T
MESS WITH ME! = ¡MA' P'U'UJSE TEEN!

¡LLAMA LA POLICÍA! / CALL THE POLICE! = ¡PAY /
PAYE'EX POLIISYA!

¡HÁGALO! / DO IT! = ¡BEETE!

ALGUIÉN ME ROBÓ / SOMEONE ROBBED ME =
JUNTUUL WIINIK TZ'OK U YOKLIKEEN IN
BA'ALO'OB

ALGUIÉN HURTÓ MIS PERTENECÍAS / SOMEONE
STOLE MY THINGS = JUUNTUL WIINIK TZ'OK U
YOKLIK IN BA'ALO'OB

¿DÓNDE ESTÁ EL HOSPITAL? / WHERE IS THE
HOSPITAL? = ¿TU'UX YAAN YOTOCH TZ'AAK?

UNA SERPIENTE ME MORDIÓ / A SNAKE BIT ME =
JUNTUUL KAAN TZ'OK U CHI'IBALEEN

UN CHUCHO ME MORDIÓ / A DOG BIT ME =
JUUNTUL PEEK' TZ'OK U CHI'IBALEEN

ESTOY SANGRANDO MUCHO / I AM BLEEDING VERY BAD = YA'AB K'I'IK' TUN JOK'OOL TEEN

NECESITO BEBER UN POCO AGUA / I NEED TO DRINK WATER = K'AABEET IN WUK'AL JUUMP'IIT JA'

ESTOY ENFERMO / I AM SICK = K'OJA'ANEEN

TENGO MUCHO DOLOR / I AM IN A LOT OF PAIN = YAAN TEEN YA'AB YAAJ

(…) ME DUELE / MY…HURTS = TUN CHI'IBAL […]

AAK' = LENGUA / TONGUE

AAL K'AB = DEDO DE MANO / FINGER

AAL OOK = DEDO DE PIE / TOE

BAK'EL IIT = TRASERO / BUTTOCKS

BOOX = LABIOS / LIPS

CHI' = BOCA / MOUTH

ICH = CARA; ROSTRO / FACE

ICH = OJO / EYE

IIT = ANO / ANUS

JO'OL = CABEZA / HEAD

K'AB = BRAZO; MANO / ARM; HAND

KELEMBAL = HOMBROS / SHOULDERS

KOJ = DIENTE / TOOTH; TEETH

NAK' = ESTOMAGO / STOMACH

NI' = NARIZ / NOSE

OOK = PIE / FOOT

P'U'UKIL IIT = TRASERO / BUTTOCKS

PAACH = ESPALDA / BACK

POOL = CABEZA / HEAD

T'UUP = MEÑIQUE / PINKY FINGER

TOON = PENE / PENIS

XIIBIL = PENE / PENIS

XIKIN = OREJA / EAR

TENGO DIARREA / I HAVE DIARRHEA = YAAN TEEN DIARREA

TENGO DIARREA Y VOMITOS / I HAVE VOMITING AND DIARRHEA = YAAN TEEN XEJ YETEL DIARREA

TENGO MIEDO / I'M AFRAID = YAAN TEEN SAJKIIL

TENÍA MIEDO / I WAS AFRAID = YAANJI TEEN SAJKIIL

NO TENGAS MIEDO / DON'T BE AFRAID = MA' YAANI TEECH SAJKIIL

LLÉVAME AL HOSPITAL / TAKE ME TO THE HOSPITAL = BIISE TEEN TI' YOTOCH TZ'AAK

V) NUMBERS

EACH NUMBER MAY RECEIVE A CLASSIFIER DEPENDING ON WHAT IS BEING COUNTED. HERE IS A SHORT LIST OF CLASSIFIERS THAT WILL BE USED WHEN COUNTING CERTAIN THINGS:

-P'EL = IN GENERAL; INANIMATE

-TZ'IIT = LONG SLENDER OBJECTS

-KUUL = TREES

-TUUL = PEOPLE OR ANIMALS; ANIMATE

EXAMPLE:

OOXKUUL CHE'OB = THREE TREES

KANTUUL MAAKOB = FOUR MEN

NUMBERS ABOVE 5 ARE USUALLY NOT USED BY SPEAKERS OF YUCATEC AND THEREFORE NUMBERS AFTER 5 ARE BASED ON THE CLASSICAL ERA EXAMPLES. 1-5 ARE COMMONLY USED TO COUNT THINGS WHILE AFTER 5, NATIVE SPEAKERS USUALLY SWITCH AND USE SPANISH NUMBERS INSTEAD OF MAYAN NUMBERS.

NUMBERS:

JUN = 1

KA'A = 2

OOX = 3

KAN = 4

JO' = 5

WAAK = 6

UK = 7

WAXAK = 8

BOLON = 9

LAJUN = 10

BULUK = 11

LAJKA'A = 12

OOX LAJUN = 13

KAN LAJUN = 14

JO' LAJUN = 15

WAK LAJUN = 16

UK LAJUN = 17

WAXAK LAJUN = 18

BOLON LAJUN = 19

JUN K'AAL = 20

JUN K'AAL JUN = 21

JUN K'AAL KA'A = 22

JUN K'AAL OOX = 23

JUN K'AAL KAN = 24

JUN K'AAL JO' = 25

JUN K'AAL WAK = 26

JUN K'AAL UK = 27

JUN K'AAL WAXAK = 28

JUN K'AAL BOLON = 29

KA' K'AAL = 40

OOX K'AAL = 60

KAN K'AAL = 80

JO' K'AAL = 100

LAJUN K'AAL = 200

JUN BAK = 400

KA' BAK = 800

Useful Yucatec Maya Vocabulary:

FOOD – O'OCH / WAAJ

ACHIOTE [SPICE] = K'UXU' / K'IWI'

AGAVE = KI

AGUARDIENTE [LIQUOR] = AANIS

ATOL = SA'

ATOL = SAKSA'

AVOCADO = OON

BANANA = JA'AS

BEAN, LIMA = IIB

BEANS = BU'UL

BEER = CHEBA

BEER, FERMENTED HONEY = BAALCHE'

BREAD = WAAJ

BROTH = K'AAB / K'AA' / K'OOL

CACAO = KAKAW

CACTUS = PAAK'AM

CANDY = CH'UJUK

CATFISH = LU'

CHICKEN = KAAX

CHICKEN, BAKED = PIIBIL KAAX

CHICKEN, FRIED = TZAJBIL KAAX

CHILE = IIK

CHOCOLATE = CHUKWA'

CIGAR = SAAK'

CIGARETTE = CHAMAL

CITRUS FRUIT = PAK'AAL

COFFEE = BOXJA'

COFFEE = KAAPE

CORN = IXIM

CORN = XI'IM

CORNMEAL = SAKAN

COW = WAKAX

CRAB = BAB

EGG = JE'

FISH = KAY

FLOUR, CORN [MASA] = SAKAN

FOOD = JAANAL

FOOD = O'OCH

FOOD = WAAJ

FRUIT = CH'UJUK

GUAVA = PICHI'

HONEY = KAAB

ICE = BAT

JICAMA [EDIBLE ROOT] = CHI'IKAM

MANGO = MAANKO

MEAL = JAANAL

MEAT = BAK'

MEAT, FRESH = AAK' BAK'

MEAT, GRILLED = K'A'BIL BAK'

MEAT, GRILLED = POK CHUK

MILE = LEECHE

ORANGE = CHIINA

ORANGE JUICE = K'AAB CHIINA

PAPAYA = PUUT

PEANUT BUTTER = MANIIYA

PEPPER = IIK

PIG = AK

PLUM = ABAL

PORK, ROASTED = PIIBIL K'EEK'EN

POSOL [CORN GRUEL] = K'EYEM

PUMPKIN = K'UUM

RICE = AROS

SALT = TA'AB

SAPOTE [REGIONAL FRUIT] = YA'

SEEDS [PEPITA] = SIKIL

SOURSOP [CUSTARD APPLE] = OOP

SQUASH = K'UUM

STEW = K'OOL

SUGAR = ASUKAAR

SWEET POTATO / YAM = IIS

TOBACCO = K'UUTZ

TOMATO = P'AAK

TORTILLA = WAAJ

TURKEY = TZ'O'

TURKEY = JTZ'O'

TURKEY = TZUN

TURKEY = ULUM

TURKEY = TUX

VENISON = KEEJ

WATER = JA'

ANIMALS – BA'ALCHE' / ALAK'

ALLIGATOR = AAYIN

ANIMAL, DOMESTIC = AALAK'

ANIMAL, WILD = BA'ALCHE'

ARMADILLO = IBACH

ARMADILLO = WECH

BAT = SOOTZ'

BAT, VAMPIRE = CHIKOOP

BEDBUG = PIK

BEE = KAAB

BIRD = CH' IICH'

BLUE JAY [BIRD] = CH' EL

BOA CONSTRICTOR = OCH KAAN

BOAR = KITAM

BULL = WAKAX

BUTTERFLY = PEEPEM

CAIMAN = AAYIN

CAT = MIIS

CATFISH = LU'

CHICKEN = KAAX

COW = WAKAX

COYOTE = CH'AMAK

COYOTE = CH'OMAK

COYOTE = JWAYU

CRAB = BAB

CROCODILE = AAYIN

DEER = KE

DEER, SMALL = YUUK

DOG = PEEK'

DOVE = XUUKUM

EAGLE = MEN

EEL = KAANILJA'

FALCON = KOOS

FISH = KAY

FLY = XYA'AXKAACH

FOX = CH'AMAK

FOX = CH'OMAK

FROG = MUUCH

GNAT = US

GOAT = JTAMAN

GRASSHOPPER = SAAK'

HEADLICE = UK'

HERON, WHITE = SAK BOK

HORSE = TZIIMIN

HUMMINGBIRD = TZ'UNU'UN

IGUANA = JOOJ

JAGUAR = BAALAM

JAGUAR = BAALAN

JAGUAR = CHAKMO'OL

JAGUAR = KO

LICE = UK'

LIZARD = IXMECH

LIZARD = JOOJ

LIZARD, SMALL = TOOLOK

LOCUST = SAAK'

LOUSE = UK'

MACAW = MO'

MONKEY = TUUCHA

MONKEY, HOWLER = BAATZ'

MONKEY, IN GENERAL = MA'AX

MOSQUITO = K'AXOL

MOSQUITO = K'OXOL

MOUNTAIN LION = KO

MOUSE = CH'O'

OWL = BUUJ

OWL = TUNKULUUCHU

OX = WAKAX

PACA, LARGE RODENT = JAALEB

PARROT = XT' UUT'

PECCARY, WILD PIG = KITAM

PIG = AK

PORCUPINE = K'I'IX PECH OOCH

PUMA = KO

QUAIL = BEECH'

QUETZAL [BIRD] = K'UK'

RABBIT = T'U'UL

RACCOON = K'ULU'

RAT = CH'O'

RATTLESNAKE = TZAA'KAAN

RATTLESNAKE = TZAAB'KAAN

ROOSTER = T'EEL

SCORPION = SIINA'AN

SHEEP = JTAMAN

SKUNK = PAAYOOCH

SNAIL = UURICH

SNAKE = KAAN

SPIDER = AM

SQUIRREL = KU'UK

TARANTULA = CHIIN WOL

TICK [INSECT] = PEECH

TOUCAN = PIITORLEEYAAL

TURKEY = TUX

TURKEY = TZ'O'

TURKEY = JTZ'O'

TURKEY = TZON

TURKEY, DOMESTICATED = UULUM

TURKEY, WILD = KUUTZ

TURTLE = AAK

VULTURE = CH'OOM

WASP = XUUX

WEASEL = OOCH

WOLF = KABKO

WORM = KAAN

WORM = NOK'OL

PEOPLE – WIINIKO'OB

BABY = CHAAMPAL

BOSS = NOOJOCHIIL

BOY = PAAL

BOY = XI'IPAL

BROTHER (BY BLOOD) = LAAK'TZIIL

BROTHER (OLDER) = SUKU'UN

BROTHER (YOUNGER) = IITZ'IIN

BROTHER (YOUNGER) = JT'UUP

CHIEF = JOLIIL

CHILD = CHAAMPAL

CHILD = PAAL

CHILD, BLONDE = CHAN CH'EL

CHILD, BLONDE OR RED-HAIRED = CHAN
CH'EL

CURER = JMEEN

DEMON (MALE) = JTAABAY

DEMON (MALE) = JTABAAY

DEMON = XTAABAY

DEMON = XTABAAY

DEVIL = KISIN

DOCTOR (FEMALE) = XTZ'AAK

DOCTOR (MALE) = JTZ'AAK

DREAMER (FEMALE) = XWAYAK'

DREAMER (MALE) = JWAYAK'

DUMMY = JNUUM

EVIL MAN = JK'AAS

EVIL WOMAN = XK'AAS

FARMER = KOOLNAAL

FATHER = PAAPA

FATHER = TAAT

FATHER = YUUM

FIGHTER = JBA'TE'EL

FOREIGNER (FEMALE) = XUNAAN

FOREIGNER = TZ'UUL

FOREST SPIRIT = YUNTZIL

FRIEND = AAMIGO

FRIEND = ET'OOL

FRIEND = UK'UNAJ WIINIK

GAY (HOMOSEXUAL) = XCH'UUPUL XIB

GENTLEMAN = YUUM

GHOST (FEMALE) = XTAABAY

GHOST (FEMALE) = XTABAAY

GHOST (MALE) = JTAABAY

GHOST (MALE) = JTABAAY

GIRL = XCH'UUPAL

GOD = DYOS

GOD = K'U

GOD = YUUM

GODS = K'UJO'OB

GRANDCHILD = AABIL

GRANDFATHER (AGED) = MAM

GRANDFATHER = NOJOCH PAAPA

GRANDFATHER = NOJOCH TAAT

GRANDFATHER = NOJOCH TAATA

GRANDMOTHER = CHIICH

HELPER = AANTAJ

HOMOSEXUAL = XCH'UUPUL XIB

HUNTER = TZ'ONERO

HUNTER = TZ'ONNAAL

HUSBAND = IICHAM

HUSBAND = JWICHAM

IDIOT = JNUUM

IGNORANT PERSON = JNUUM

IMBECIL = JNUUM

INDIAN = JMAYABIIL

INDIAN = MAASEWAAL

INDIGENOUS PERSON = JMAYABIIL

INDIGENOUS PERSON = MAASEWAAL

INFANT = PAAL

INJURED MAN = JLOOB

INJURED WOMAN = XLOOB

LADY = XUNAAN

LAZY MAN = JOYKEEP

LOCAL PERSON = WAYILE'

MAIDEN = SUJUY PAAL

MALE = XIIB

MAN = MAAK

MAN = WIINIK

MAN = XIIB

MEDICINE MAN = JMEEN

MEXICAN (FEMALE) = XWAACH

MEXICAN (MALE) = JWAACH

MINOR = PAAL

MOTHER = MAAM

MOTHER = NA'

NATIVE = WAYILE'

OLD MAN = NOJOCH WIINIK

OLD MAN = NUXIIB

OLD WOMAN = NOJOCH KO'OLEL

OLD WOMAN = XNUUK

OWNER = YUUM

PARENT = LAAK

PERSON = MAAK

PERSON = WIINIK

POPE = PAAPA

PRIEST = AJK'IIN

PRIEST = JK'IIN

QUEER (HOMOSEXUAL) = XCH'UUPUL XIIB

RELATIVE = CHILANKABIL

RELATIVE = LAAK'

SAINTS = K'UJO'OB

SALESMAN = KOONOL

SALESWOMAN = XKOONOL

SHAMAN = JMEEN

SIBLING (FEMALE) = LAAK'TZIIL

SIBLING (MALE) = JK'EBAN

SISTER (OLDER) = KIIK

SISTER (YOUNGER) = IITZ'IIN

SISTER (YOUNGER) = XT'UUP

SOLDIER = JK'ATUN

SOLDIER = K'ATUN

SOLDIER = WAACH

SOMEONE = WAAJ MAAX

SON = PAAL

SPEAKER (FEMALE) = XT'AN

SPEAKER (MALE) = JT'AN

SPOUSE = LAAK'

STEP-FATHER = MAJAN YUUM

STRANGER (FEMALE) = XUNAAN

STRANGER (MALE) = TZ'UUL

STUPID MAN = JNUUM

STUPID WOMAN = XNUUM

TEACHER = KA'ANSAJ

VENDOR (FEMALE) = XKOONOL

VENDOR (MALE) = KOONOL

VIRGEN (WOMAN) = SUJUY PAAL

VIRGIN = SUJUY

WHITE MAN = TZ'UUL

WHITE WOMAN = XUNAAN

WIFE = ATAN

WITCH = XWAAY

WIZARD = JWAAY

WOMAN = KO'OLEL

WOMAN = XCH'UUP

WORKER = JMEYAJ

WRITER (FEMALE) = XTZ'IIB

WRITER (MALE) JTZ'IIB

YOUNG WOMAN = SUJUY PAAL

YOUTH = XI'IPAAL

PLACES – KAAJTALO'OB

BANK = BAANKO

BATHROOM = BAANYO

CHURCH = IGLEESYA

CHURCH = YOTOCH DYOS

FIELD = KOL

FOREST = K'AAX

HEAVEN = KA'AN

HOME = OTOCH

HOUSE = KAJTAL

HOUSE = OTOCH

JAIL = KARSA

JAIL = KARSE

LAND = KAAB

LAND = LU'UM

MOUNTAINS = WITZOB

PLACE = KAJTAL

RESTROOM = BAANYO

ROAD = BEEL

SKY = KA'AN

TOWN = KAJ

TOWN = NOJKAJ

VALLEY = K'OM

VALLEY = K'OP

VILLAGE = KAJ

VILLAGE = NOJKAJ

WORLD = KAAB

NATURE – LE LU'UMO'

AIR = IIK'

AREA = BAANDA

BARK (TREE) = SOOL

CEIBA [REGIONAL TREE] = YAXCHE'

CLOUD = MUNYAL

CYCLONE = CHAKIK'AT

DAWN = SAASTAL

DAY = K'IIN

DEW = YEEB

DUSK = BIN KA AK'ABTAL

EARTH = KAAB

EARTH = LU'UM

EAST = LAK'IN

FIELD = KOL

FIRE = K'AAK'

FIREWOOD = SI'

FLOWER = LOOL

FLOWER = NIKTE'

FOG = YEEB

FOREST = K'AAX

FOUNTAIN = SAYAB

HAIL = BAT

HILL = MUUL

LAGOON = AAK'AL

LAKE = JA'

LANDMARK = XU'UK

LEAF = LE'

MIST = YEEB

MOON = UW

MOUNTAIN = WITZ

MOUNTAINS = WITZOB

NIGHT = AK'AB

NORTH = XAMAN

NORTH WIND = XAMAN KA'AN

PLANT = PAK'AL

RAIN = CHAAK

RAIN = JA'

RIVER = BEKAN

ROCK = TUUNICH

ROOT = MOOTZ

ROSE = LOOL

SOIL = LU'UM

SOUTH = NOJOL

STONE = TUUNICH

SUN = K'IIN

SWAMP = AAK'AL

THUNDER = JUUM CHAAK

TREE = CHE'

TREE, CEIBA [REGIONAL TREE] = YAXCHE'

TWIG = CH'ILIB

VALLEY = K'OM

VALLEY = K'OP

VINE = AAK'

VIRGIN FOREST = SUJUY K'AAX

WEED = K'AAX

WEST = CHIK'IN

WIND = IIK'

WOOD = CHE'

WORLD = KAAB

WORLD = LU'UM

OTHER IMPORTANT WORDS – LAAK'
K'A'ANA'AN T'AANOB

ABILITY = PAT

ACCIDENT = LOOB

AFFAIR = BEEL

AGE = JA' ABIIL

ALTAR = KA'ANCHE'

AX = BAAT

BAG = SAABUKAAN

BALL = PELOOTA

BASE = CHUUN

BASE = IIT

BASE = JAAL

BASKET, LARGE = XUUX

BASKET, SMALL = XAAK

BEAUTY = JATZ'UTZIIL

BEGINNING = CHUUN

BIT = XEET'

BLOW [WITH FIST] = LOOBIIL

BOAT = CHEEM

BOOK = JU'UN

BOX = PIIX

BROOM = MIIS

BUCKET = CH'OOY

BUILDING = NAJIIL

BURDEN = KUUCH

CANDLE = KIB

CANOE = CHEM

CAR = KAARO

CASE = PIIX

CHARCOAL = CHUUK

COLD MEDICINE = TZ'AAK SE'EN

COMB = XAACHE'

COTTON = TAMAN

DANCE = OOK'OT

DIGNITY = SU'TAL

DISTANCE = NAACHIIL

DOLL = AALNOOK'

DREAM = WAYAK'

DYE = BON

EDGE = CHI'

EDGE = EJ

EDGE = JAAL

EMBARASSMENT = SU'UTAL

END = TZ'OOK

END = XUUL

ENERGY = OOL

ENGLISH LANGUAGE = INGLES

ENTRANCE = JOOL

ERRAND = TUS BEEL

ERROR = SI'IPIIL

ERROR = SIIP

EXCREMENT = TA'

EXPLANATION = NU'UKUL

FALSEHOOD = TUUS

FART = KIIS

FAULT (BLAME) = KUUCH

FAULT (BLAME) = SI'IPIIL

FAULT (BLAME) = SIIP

FAVOR = UTZIIL

FEAR = SAJKIIL

FECES = TA'

FIGHT = BA'TE'EL

FIRE = K'AAK'

FIREWOOD = SI'

FLATULENCE = KIIS

FLINT = TOK' TUUNICH

FLUTE = PIITO

FOAM = YOON

GIFT = SIIJBIL

GOD = YUUM

GODS = K'UJO'OB

GOLD = TAAK'IN

GOODNESS = JATZ'UTZIIL

GUN = TZ'OON

HAMMOCK = K'AAN

HATCHET = BAAT

HOUR = K'IIN

HOUR = OORA

ILLNESS = K'OJA'ANIIL

INCLINE = NIIX

INJURY = LOOB

IRON = MAASKAB

ITCH = SAAK'

KEY = YAABE

KITCHEN = K'OOBEN

LABOR = MEYAJ

LANGUAGE = T'AAN

LAUGHTER = CHE'EJ

LIE = TUUS

LIFE = KUXTAL

LIGHT = K'AAK'

LIGHT = SAASIL

LOAD = KUUCH

LORD = YUUM

LOVE = YAAMAJ

MACHETE = MAASKAB

MARIJUANA = K'UUTZ

MASONRY = PAK'

MATTER = BEEL

MEDICATION = TZ'AAK

MEDICINE = TZ'AAK

MILL = JUCH'

MIRROR = NEEN

MISFORTUNE = LOOB

MONEY = TAAK'IN

MOVEMENT = PEEK

MUSIC = K'AAY

NAME = K'ABA'

NAPKIN = JAAY

NEEDLE = PUUTZ'

NEST = K'U'

NIGHTMARE = K'AAS WAYAK'

NOTHING = MIXBA'AL

OBLIGATION = KUUCH

ODOR = CH'E'J

OMEN = TAMAX CHI'

OPENING = CHI'

OPENING = JOOL

PAIN = K'I'INAM

PAINT = BON

PAPER = JU'UN

PIECE = XEET'

PILLAR = OKOM

PILLOW = XK'AANJO'OL

POINT = U YEJ

POLE = CHE'

PORTION = XEET'

POST = OKOM

PRICE = TOJOL

PROBLEM = BA'TE'EL

PYRAMID = MUUL

REASON = NU'UKUL

RESERVOIR = AAK'AL

ROAD = BEEL

ROOF = U JO'OL NAJ

ROOF = U POOL NAJ

ROPE = SUUM

RUST = ITZ

SAINTS = K'UJO'OB

SAP = ITZ

SHADE = BO'OY

SHADOW = BO'OY

SHAME = SU'UTAL

SHELL (EGG) = SOOL

SHIT = TA'

SHOTGUN = TZ'OON

SHOW = CHA'AN

SICKNESS = K'OJA'ANIIL

SIN = K'EBAN

SIN = SI'IPIIL

SIN = SIIP

SINKHOLE = TZ'OONO'OT

SITUATION = BEEL

SIZE = NOJOCHIIL

SLOPE = NIIX

SMELL = BOK

SMOKE = BUUTZ'

SNARE = PEETZ'

SONG = K'AAY

SOUND = JUUM

SOURCE = SAYAB

SPANISH LANGUAGE = KAXLANT'AAN

SPARK = XIKIN K'AAK'

SPECTACLE = CHA'AN

SPEECH = T'AAN

STAR = EEK'

STEM = CHUN

STICK = CHE'

STING = AACH

STOOL = K'AANCHE'

STORM = CHIICHIK'

STRAP = K'AXAB NAK'

STRAW = SIIT

STRENGTH = MUUK'

TABLE = MEESA

THICKNESS = POOLKIIL

THING = BA'AL

THORN = K'I'IX

THOUGHT = TUUKUL

TIME = K'IIN

TOBACCO = K'UUTZ

TOOL = NU'UKUL

TOOTHPICK = CH'ILIB

TOWEL = TWAAYA

TRAP = PEETZ'

TRASH = SOJOL

TRUTH = JAAJIIL

URINE = WIIX

UTENSIL = NU'UKUL

VALUE = TOJOL

VOICE = KAAL

VOMIT = XEJ

WART = AAX

WASHTUB = CHEEM

WEEK = SAMAANA

WHISTLE = PIITO

WILL = OOL

WINDOW = WENTANA

WOOD = CHE'

WORK = MEYAJ

WORK = OOBRA

WOUND = LOOB

WRITING = TZ'IIB

YEAR = AANYO

YEAR =JA'ABIIL

COMMON ADJECTIVES

ACCUSTOMED = SUUK

ACIDIC = PAJ

ALIVE = KUXA'AN

ANCIENT = UUCHBEN

ANGERED = P'UJUUL

ASHAMED = SU'LAK

BAD = K'AAS

BEAUTIFUL = JATZ'UTZ

BIG = NOJOCH

BITTER = K'AAJ

BLIND = CH'OP

BOTHERED = P'UJUUL

BROKEN = KAACHA'AL

BUSTED = KAACHA'AL

CAPTURED = CHUKA'AN

CHANGED = K'EEXEL

CHEAP = MA' KO'OJI'

CLEAN = JAANIL

CLEAN = SAK

CLEAR = SAAS

CLOUDY = NOOKOY

COLD = SIIS

CONSUMED = XUUPUL

CONTENT = KI'IMAK OOL

CONVENIENT = KI'

COOKED = TAK'AN

CROSSED = K'AATAL

CROWDED = BABAJKIL

CUTE = JATZ'UTZ

DANGEROUS = JACH K'AAS U BIN

DARK = EE'JOCH'E'EEN

DEAD = KIMEN

DEAF = KOOK

DEEP = TAAM

DELICATE = LUKUM

DIFFERENT = JEEL

DIFFERENT = JELA'AN

DIFFICULT = YAJ

DIRTY = EEK'

DISTANT = NAACH

DISTINCT = JELA'AN

DONE = TZ'OKA'AN

DRIED = JAYK'INTA'AN

DRUNK = KALA'AN

DRY = TIKIN

DUMB = TZ'U'UY POOL

EMBARASSED = SU'LAK

ENOUGH = JACH YA'AB

EVIL = K'AAS

EXCHANGED = K'EEXEL

EXPENSIVE = KO'OJ

EXPLODED = WAAK'AL

EXTENDED = TIINIL

FADED = POOS

FAIR (PERSON) = CHAKXICH'

FAIR (COMPLEXIONED) = CH'EL

FAT = POLOK

FILLED = CHUUPUL

FINE = LUKUM

FINISHED = CHUKA'AN

FINISHED = TZ'OKA'AN

FIRST = YAAXIIL

FIXED = JETZ'A'AN

FLAT = PEK'A'AN

FORCEFUL = JELA'AN

FRACTURED = KAACHA'AL

FRIED = TZAJBIL

FRIGHTENED = P'UUJUL

FULL = CHUUP

GOOD = MA'ALOB

GOOD = UTZ

GOOD-LOOKING = KI'ICHPAM

GOOFY = NUUM

GOOFY = TZ'U'UY POOL

GRILLED = K'A'BIL

GROUND (UP) = JUCH'BIL

HALF = CHUMUK

HANDSOME = JATZ'UTZ

HANDSOME = KI'ICHPAM

HAPPY = KI'IMAK OOL

HARSH = K'A'AM

HEATED UP = K'IINAL

HEAVY = AL

HIGH = KA'ANAL

HOARSE = MA'A KAAL

HOLLOW = POOS

HOT (FOOD; SPICY) = PAAP

HOT (WEATHER) = K'IILKAB

HOT = CHOKOJ

HOT = K'IINAL

HUMBLE = UMIILDE

HUNGRY = WI'IJ

IGNORANT = NUUM

IMPORTANT = K'A'ANA'AN

INDIGENOUS = MAASEWAAL

INTACT = SUJUY

INTOXICATED = KALA'AN

JUST = UTZ

LARGE (PLURAL) = NUKUCH

LARGE = NOJOCH

LAZY = NUUM

LEATHERY = TZ'U'UY

LEFT = TZ'IK

LIGHT = SAAL

LITTLE = CHAN

LITTLE = MA' YA'ABI'

LITTLE = MEJEN

LIVING = KUXA'AN

LONG = CHOWAK

LOST = SAATAL

LOUD = CH'E'EJ

LOW = KAABAL

MANY = YA'AB

MANY = YA'AKACH

MARRIED = TZ'OKA'AN BEEL

MATURE = TAK'AN

MOIST = CH'UUL

MUDDY = PUUK

NAKED = CHAKNUL

NARROW = KOOM

NEAR = NAATZ'

NEW = TUMBEN

NICE = JATZ'UTZ

NICE = KI'

NICE = LUKUM

NICE, VERY = SEN UTZ

NOISY = CH'E'EJ

OBSCURE = EE'JOCH'E'EEN

OLD = CH'IJA'AN

OLD = NOJOCH

OLD = NUXIB

OLD = UUCHBEN

OPENED = JE'AN

OPENED = JE'IK

OPENED = JEBAN

OTHER = JEEL

OTHER = LAAK'

OVERCAST = NOOKOY

PAINFUL = YAJ

PAINTED = BO'ON

PAINTED = BOONOL

PREGNANT = YO'OM

PRETTY = JATZ'UTZ

PRETTY = KI'ICHPAM

QUICK = SEEBAK

RICH = AYIK'AL

RICH = TAAK'INAL

RIPE = K'AN

RIPE = TAK'AN

ROASTED = K'A'BIL

ROUND = WOLIS

SCRAMBLED = PUUK'

SEATED = JETZ'A'AN

SEATED = KULA'AN

SECONDHAND = ASBE'EN

SECURED = JETZ'A'AN

SETTLED = JETZ'A'AN

SHAVEN = TZ'IKA'AN

SICK = K'OJA'AN

SILLY = NUUM

SINGLE = JUN

SKINNY = TZ'OYA'AN

SLICED = TAAJAL

SLIPPERY = JAJALKIL

SLOW = CHAAMBEEL

SMALL = CHAN

SMALL = CHICHAN

SMALL = MEJEN

SMOOTH = JOJOLKIL

SMOOTH = TAAX

SOUR = PAJ

SPICY = PAAP

SPILLED = WEEJEL

SPILLED = WEEKEL

SPLIT = KAACHA'AL

STIFF = T'IINIL

STILL (NOT MOVING) = WA'BAL

STOLEN = OOKOLBIL

STOPPED = WA'BAL

STRAIGHT = TOJ

STRANGE = JELA'AN

STRONG = CHICH

STRONG = K'A'AM

STUPID = NUUM

STUPID = TZ'U'UY POOL

SUBMERGED = T'UBUKBAL

SUBMERGED = T'UUBAL

SUBSTITUTED = K'EEXEL

SUFFICIENT = JACH YA'AB

SUNKEN = T'UBUKBAL

SUNKEN = T'UUBAL

SUPER = SEN MA'ALOB

SURPRISING = JAK'OOLAL

SWEET = CH'UJUK

SWOLLEN = CHUUP

TAME = SUUK

TASTY = KI'

TENSE = T'IINIL

THICK = PIIM

THICK = POLOK

THIN (PAPER / CLOTHES) = JAAY

THIN = BEK'ECH

THIRSTY = UK'AJ

TILTED = NIIXIL

TIRED = KA'ANA'AN

TOASTED = POKBIL

TOO MANY = JACH YA'AB

TOUGH = CHICH

TOUGH = TZ'U'UY

TRUE = JAAJ

UNTIDY = LOOB

USED = ASBE'EN

USED UP = XU'UPI

USELESS = NUUM

VERY = JACH

WASHED = P'O'A'AL

WEALTHY = AYIK'AL

WET = CH'UUL

WIDE = KOOCH

WILD = K'O'OX

WRONG = K'EBAN

THE BODY – LE WIINKILO'

ANUS = IIT

ARM = K'AB

BACK = PAACH

BEAK (BIRD) = KO

BEARD = ME'EX

BELLY = NAK'

BONE = BAK

BOSOM = IIM

BREAST = IIM

BUTT = BAK'EL IIT

BUTT = P'U'UKIL IIT

BUTTOCKS = BAK'EL IIT

BUTTOCKS = P'U'UKIL IIT

CALLUS = T'AAJAM

CHIN = K'O NO'OCH

CLAW (ANIMAL) = IICH'AK

CLITORIS = AK'

EAR = XIKIN

EXCREMENT = TA'

EYE = ICH

FACE = ICH

FANG (ANIMAL) = TZ'A'AY

FAT = TZAATZ

FEATHERS (BIRD) = K'U'UK'UM

FINGER = AAL K'AB

FINGER = U YAAL K'AB

FINGERNAIL = IICH'AK

FLESH = BAK'

FOOT = OOK

HAIR = JO'OL

HAIR = TZO'OTZ

HAIR = U TZO'OTZ A JO'OL

HAND = K'AB

HEAD = JO'OL

HEART = OOL

HEART = PUKSI'IK'AL

HEEL = TUUNKUY

HORN (ANIMAL) = BAK

INTESTINES = CHOOCH

KNEE = PIIX

LIPS = BOOX

LIVER = TAAMAN

MOUSTACHE = ME'EX

MOUTH = CHI'

MUCUS = SIIM

NAIL = IICH'AK

NECK = KAAL

NERVE = XIICH'

NOSE = NI'

PENIS = TOON

PENIS = XIIBIL

PUS = TZ'IIK

RUMP = BAK'EL IIT

SHOULDER = KELEMBAL

SINEW = XIICH'

SKIN = K'EEWEL

SOUL = PIXAAN

STOMACH = NAK'

TAIL (ANIMAL) = NE

TEAT = IIM

TENDON = XIICH'

TESTICLES = U YE'EL TOON

THROAT = KAAL

TOE = AAL OOK

TONGUE = AK'

TOOTH; TEETH = KO

URINE = WIIX

VOICE = KAAL

VOMITE = XE

WING (BIRD) = XIIK'

CLOTHING – NOOK'

BELT = K'AXAB NAK'

CAPE = JAAY

CLOAK = JAAY

CLOTH = NOOK'

CLOTHES = NOOK'

CLOTHING = NOOK'

FABRIC = NOOK'

FOOTWEAR = XANAB

HAT = P'OK

HAT, MADE FROM STRAW = XA'ANIL P'OK

HUIPIL [TRADITIONAL DRESS FOR WOMEN] = IIPIL

LEATHER = K'EEWEL

PANTS = EEX

SANDAL = XANAB

SHAWL = BOOCH'

SHIRT = KAMIISA

SHOE = XANAB

SHOES = XANAB

T-SHIRT = KAMIISA

UNDERWEAR = EEX

COLORS – KOLORILO'OB

BLACK = BOX

BLACK = EEK'

BLUE = YA'AX

BROWN = MORENO

GREEN = YA'AX

ORANGE = ANARANJADO

PINK = CHAKPOSE'EN

PURPLE = MORADO

RED = CHAK

WHITE = SAK

YELLOW = K'AN

COMMON VERBS

EXAMPLE: LOVE = YAKUNTIK

NOTES:

-VERBS WITH THE -IK SUFFIX ATTACHED TO THE ROOT ARE ALWAYS TRANSITIVE VERBS

-VERBS WITHOUT A SUFFIX ATTACHED TO THE ROOT ARE ALMOST ALWAYS INTRANSITIVE

-VERBS WITH THE -TAL ENDING, WILL RECEIVE -TAL VERB CONJUGATION (SEE VERB SECTION GRAMMAR)

ABANDON = NAK'

ACCEPT A PROPOSITION = KETIK

ADD = TZAKBESAJ

ADJUST = NUUKBESAJ

ADORN = SENBESAJ

 AGE = CH'IIJ

ALLOW = CHA'

ALLOW = CHA'IK

AMUSE = BAAXAL

ANSWER = NUUKIK

APPROACH = NAATZ'AL

APPROACH = NAATZ'IK

ARISE = LIIK'IL

ARRIVE = K'UCHUL

ASK FOR = K'AATIK

ATTAIN = CHUKIK

AWAKEN = AJAL

BAKE = TAJAL

BATHE = ICHKIIL

BE = YAAN

BE ABLE TO = PAAJTAL (*AUXILIARY*)

BE BORN = SIIJIL

BE HUNGRY = WI'IJ- + SET B AFFIX

BE LATE = XANAL

BE MARRIED = TZ'OKA'AN BEEL

BE SUSPENDED = CH'UUYUL

BE THIRSTY = UK'AJ- +SET B AFFIX

BEAT (MIXING INGREDIENTS) = P'UUCH

BEAT (WITH FISTS) = JATZ'IK

BECOME ACCUSTOMED = NAPTZAAJ

BECOME CLOUDY = NOOKOYTAL

BECOME DENSE = SU'UTAL

BECOME DRUNK = KAALTAL

BECOME HOT = CHOKOTAL

BECOME ILL = K'OJA'ANTAL

BECOME OVERCAST = NOOKOYTAL

BECOME PREGNANT = YO'OMCHAJTAL

BECOME WET = CH'ULCHAJTAL

BEGIN = CHUUNIK

BEGIN = KAAJSIK

BEND = WUTZ'IK

BITE = CHI'IBAL

BLESS = BENDISYONTIK

BLOCK (ROAD) = SUP'IK

BLOW (WITH MOUTH) = USTIK

BOIL = TAJAL

BOTHER = P'U'UJSIK

BOUNCE = SIIT'

BREAK (LONG THINGS) = KACHIK

BREAK (OUT IN RASH) = IXBAL

BREAK SOMETHING = PA'IK

BREAK SOMETHING = XIKIK

BREAKFAST (TO HAVE BREAKFAST) = UK'UL

BREATHE = CH'A'IIK

BREATHE = CH'A'IK IIK

BRING = TAASIK

BRUISE = PUCH'IK

BURN = ELEL

BURN = TOK

BURN = TOOKIK

BURST = XIKIK

BUY = MANIK

CAN (TO BE ABLE) = KU' PAAJTAL

CAN = JU' CHABALE

CARE FOR = KANANTIK

CARRY (SOMETHING ON BACK) = KUCHIK

CATCH = CHUKIK

CHANGE = K'EXIK

CHAT = TZIKBAL

CHAT = TZIKBATIK

CHEW SOMETHING = JACH'IK

CLEAN = MISTIK

CLEAN = UTZKINTIK

CLEAR = PAAK

CLIMB = NA'AKAL

CLOSE = K'ALIK

CLOSE = SUP'IK

COLLECT (FIREWOOD) BEETIK SI'

COMB (ONE'S HAIR) = XAACHTIK

COME = TAAL

COME = TAALEL

COME OUT = JOOK'OL

COMPLETE = CHUKBESIK

COOK = TAJAL

COPULATE = TZ'IIS

COUGH = SE'EN

COUNT = XOK

COUNT = XOKIK

COVER = TO'IK

CRACK = XIKIK

CROSS = K'AATEL

CRUSH = PUCH'IK

CRY = OK'OL

CURSE = MALDISYONTIK

CUT (FRUIT OR LEAVES ON A STEM) = T'OKIK

CUT = XOTIK

CUT FIREWOOD = XOTIK SI'

CUT IT WITH ONE SWING = CH'AKIK

CUT WITH SCISSORS = K'OSIK

DANCE = OK'OT

DECEIVE = KECHTIK

DECEIVE = TUUS

DECEIVE = TUUSIK

DELAY = XAANTAL

DELIVER = K'UBIK

DESCEND = EEMEL

DESIRE = TAAK (*AUXILIARY*)

DESIRE = TZ'IIBOLTIK

DETAIN = PETZ'IK

DETEST = P'EKTIK

DIE = KIIMIL

DIG = PAANIK

DIMINISH = JATZIK

DISAPPEAR = SATPAJAL

DISCUSS = TZIKBATIK

DISLIKE = P'EKTIK

DISROBE = PITIK

DISTRIBUTE = T'OXIK

DIVIDE = JATZIK

DO = BEETIK

DOMESTICATE = AALAK'TIK

DREAM = NAAY

DREAM = WAYAK'

DRENCH = CH'ULIK

DRESS ONESELF = BUUKINTIK

DRINK = UK'UL

DRY = TIIJIL

DRY = TIJSIK

EAT = JAANAL

EAT SOMETHING = JAANTIK

EMBRACE = MEEK'IK

ENTER = OOKOL

ESCAPE = PUUTZ'UL

EXCHANGE = K'EXIK

EXPECT = PA'ATIK

EXPLAIN = TZOLIK

EXPLODE = XIKIK

EXPOSE = WAK

EXTEND = SATZ'IK

EXTINGUISH = TUPIK

EXTRACT = JO'OSIK

FALL = LUUBUL

FART = KIIS

FEED = TZEENTIK

FEEL = U'UYIK

FIGHT = BA'TE'EL

FILL = BUT'IK

FILL = CHUPIK

FIND = KAXTIK

FIND OUT = OJELTIK

FINISH = CHUKBESIK

FINISH = TZ'O'OKSIK

FIX = UTZKIINTIK

FLATTEN = MACH'

FLATTEN = PAK'ACHTIK

FOLD = WUTZ'IK

FOLLOW = TZAYNEJ

FOOL SOMEONE = KECHTIK

FORGET = TU'UB

FORGET = TU'UBSIK

FORGET = TU'UBUL

FRACTURE (LONG THINGS) = KACHIK

FREE = CHA'

FREEZE = SIISKUNTIK

FRY = TZAJIK

GATHER = T'OKIK

GET AWAY = PUUTZ'UL

GET DRUNK = KALTAL

GET IN SOMETHING = NA'AKAL

GET ON SOMETHING = NA'AKAL

GIVE = TZ'IIK

GIVE AS A GIFT = SIIJIK

GIVE BACK = SUUTIK

GO = BIN (IRREGULAR)

GO = JOOK'OL

GO = XIIMBAL

GO ACROSS = K'AATEL

GO OUT = JOOK'OL

GRAB = MACHIK

GRASP = MACHIK

GRILL = K'A'ATIK

GRIND = PUCH'IK

GRIND SOMETHING = JUCH'IK

GROW = AALAK'TIK

HANG = CH'UYTAL

HANG SOMETHING = CH'UUYUL

HAPPEN = UUCHUL

HARVEST = JOOCHIK

HATE = P'EKTIK

HAVE = YAAN

HEAL = TZ'AKIK

HEAR = U'UYIK

HEAT = CHOKOKUNTIK

HELP = AANTAJ

HELP SOMEONE = AANTIK

HIDE = TA'AKIK

HIT = JATZ'IK

HUG = MEEK'IK

HUMILIATE ONESELF = TA'IK U BA

HUNT = TZ'ONIK

HURRY = SEEB

HURRY = SEEKUNTIK

HURT (INJURE) = KINBESIK

HURT = CHI'IBAL

HURT ONESELF = KINPAJAL

IGNITE = T'ABIK

IMAGINE = TZ'IIBOLTIK

IMPROVE = UTZKIINTIK

INSERT = OKSIK

INTRODUCE = OKSIK

JOKE; TELL JOKES = BAAXAL

JUMBLE = XA'AK'TIK

KEEP = KIINSIK

KISS = TZ'U'UTZ'IK

KNOW SOMEONE = K'AAJOOL

KNOW SOMEONE = K'AAJOOLTIK

KNOW SOMETHING = KANIK

KNOW SOMETHING = OOJELTIK

KNOW SOMETHING = WOJEL

LAUGH = CHE'EJ

LEAN = TOKIK

LEARN = KANIK

LEAVE = JOOK'OL

LEAVE = LUK'UL

LEND = MAJAANTIK

LET = CHA'

LIE [TELL LIES] = TUUS

LIE DOWN = CHILTAL

LIE TO SOMEONE = TUUSIK

LIFT = U'UYIK

LIVE = KAAJTAL

LOOK = PAKTIK

LOOK FOR = KAXTIK

LOOSEN = CHA'

LOSE = SATIK

LOVE = YAKUNTIK

LOWER = EENSIK

MAKE (BY HAND) = MAK'ANTIK

MAKE = BEETIK

MAKE = MENTIK

MAKE BETTER = UTZKIINTIK

MAKE READY = LI'SIK

MAKE TORTILLAS = PAK'ACH

MAKE TORTILLAS = PAK'ACHTIK

MARRY = TZ'O'OKOL BEEL

MASH = PUCH'IK

MATURE = TAJ

MEASURE = P'ISIK

MEND = UTZKIINTIK

MIX UP = XA'AK'TIK

MOISTEN = CH'ULIK

MOVE = PEEKSIK

MOVE ONESELF = PEEK

NEED = YAAN + SET A AFFIX + VERB

NOTICE = OOJELTIK

NOURISH = TZEENTIK

OFFER = WAK

OPEN = JEEB

OPEN = JEEBIK

ORDER = TUSBELTIK

ORDER; PUT IN ORDER = TZOLIK

OVERTAKE = CHUKPACHTIK

PACK = BUT'IK

PAINT = BONIK

PASS = MANSIK

PASS BY = MAAN

PASS THROUGH = POTIK

PAY = BO'OTIK

PENETRATE = POTIK

PERCEIVE = U'UYIK

PERMIT = CHA'IK

PISS = BEETIK WIIX

PLACE; PUT = TZ'IIK

PLANT = PAK'AL

PLANT = PAK'IK

PLAY = BAAXAL

PALY = BAAXTIK

POLISH = YUULTIK

POUND = PAK'ACHTIK

PRAY = BO'OTIK DYOS

PREPARE = LI'SIK

PROTECT = TA'AKIK

PULL = KOOLIK

PULL = PAAYTIK

PUNCH = LOXIK

PURSUE = CHUKPACHTIK

PUT = TZ'IIK

PUT CLOTHES ON = BUUKINTIK

PUT IN ORDER = TZOLIK

PUT OUT (FIRE, LIGHT) = TUPIK

RAIN = BEETIK CHAAK

RAIN = BEETIK JA'

RAISE (CHILD) = TZEENTIK

RAISE (LIFT) = LI'ISIK

READ = XOKIK

READ = XOOK

REAR (CHILD) = TZEENTIK

RECEIVE = K'AMIK

RECOGNIZE = K'AAJOOLTIK

RECOUNT = TZIKBATIK

RELEASE = CHA'

RELIEVE = UTZKIINTIK

REMAIN; STAY = P'AATAL

REPAIR = UTZKIINTIK

REPRIMAND = K'EYIK

RESIDE = KAAJTAL

REST = JE'ELEL

RETURN = SUUT

RETURN SOMETHING = SUUTIK

RIPEN = TAJ

RISE = LIIK'IL

ROAST = K'A'ATIK

ROB = OKLIK

ROB = OKOOL

ROLL = KOPIK

ROLL UP = TO'IK

RUB = YUULTIK

RUN = AALKAB

SALT = TA'ABIK

SAVE = TA'AKIK

SAY = A'AL

SAY SOMETHING = T'ANIK

SAY SOMETHING TO SOMEONE = A'ALIK

SCARE = P'U'UJSIK

SCOLD = K'EYIK

SCRAPE = PAANIK

SCREW = KOPIK

SEARCH = KAXTIK

SEE = ILIK

SEEK = KAXTIK

SELL = KONIK

SEND = TUUXTIK

SEW = CHUUY

SHAKE = PEEKSIK

SHAKE = TIIT

SHAKE = TIITIK

SHARE = T'OXIK

SHAVE ONESELF = TZ'IKIK

SHIT = BEETIK TA'

SHOOT = TZ'ONIK

SHOW = E'ESIK

SHOW ONESELF = E'ESIK U BA

SHUCK CORN = OXO'ONTIK

SIGNAL (WITH HAND) = PAAYK'AB

SING = K'AAY

SIT = KULAL

SIT DOWN = KULTAL

SLEEP = WENEL

SLICE = TAJ

SMASH = PETZ'IK

SMELL = U'UYIK

SMOKE A CIGARETTE OR CIGAR = TZ'U'UTZ'IK

SOW = PAK'AL

SOW = PAK'IK

SPEAK = T'AAN

SPEAK = T'AANIK

SPEAK TO SOMEONE = TZIIKBATIK

SPILL = WEKIK

SPILL WATER = WEKIK JA'

SPY = CH'UUK

STAND = WA'AK U BA

STAND UP = WA'AL

START (A FIGHT) = KETIK

STARTED; GET STARTED = CHUNPAJAL

STAY = P'AATAL

STEAL = OKLIK

STEAL = OOKOL

STICK AROUND = XAANTAL

STOP = WA'AL

STRETCH = SATZ'IK

STRIKE = JATZ'IK

STUDY = XOKIK

SUBMERGE = T'UBIK

SUBSTITUTE = K'EXIK

SUCK = TZ'U'UTZ'

SUCK = TZ'U'UTZ'IK

SUPPORT = TZEENTIK

SUSPEND = CH'UYTAL

SWALLOW = LUUK'

SWEEP = MIISTIK

SWIM = BAAB

TAKE (CARRY SOMETHING) = BIISTIK

TAKE A PHOTO = MENTIK POTO

TAKE AWAY = JATZIK

TAKE CARE OF = KANANTIK

TAKE OUT = JO'OSIK

TEACH = KA'ANSIK

TELL JOKES = BAAXAL

TELL JOKES = BAAXTIK

THERE IS / ARE = YAAN

THICKEN = SU'UTAL

THINK = TUUKUL

THROB = PEEK

THROW = CH'INIK

THROW STONES = CH'INIK

TIE = K'AXIK

TILT = NIIXIK

TIRE = KA'ANAL

TRICK = KECHTIK

TWIST = KOPIK

UNDERSTAND = NA'ATIK

UNDERSTAND = OOJELTIK

UNTIE = WACH'IK

URINATE = WIIX

USE = BAAXTIK

USE = CH'A'IK

VISIT = XIIMBATIK

VOMIT = XEJ

WAIT = PA'AT

WAIT FOR = PA'ATIK

WALK = XIIMBAL

WANT = K'AAT (*AUXILIARY*)

WASH = P'O'IK

WAVE (WITH HAND) = PAAYK'AB

WEAVE = WAK'IK

WEED; PULL WEEDS = PAAK

WEED; PULL WEEDS = PAAKTIK

WEEP = OK'OL

WEIGH = P'ISIK

WHIP = JATZ'IK

WHISTLE = XUUXUB

WISH = TZ'IIBOLTIK

WORK = MEYAJ

WORK FAST = AALKAB MEYAJ

WRAP = TO'IK

WRINKLE = CH'UKIK

WRITE = TZ'IIB

WRITE = TZ'IIBTIK

MGRNB: E^9

DISCLAIMER: